In Search of the Ultimate Goal of Life

Śrī Rāmānanda Samvāda

Śrī Śrī Guru Gaurāṅga Jayataḥ!

In Search of the Ultimate Goal of Life

Śrī Rāmānanda Samvāda

His Divine Grace
A. C. Bhaktivedānta Swāmī Prabhupāda

GOSAI PUBLISHERS

Inquiries, addressed to the secretary
of the publishers, are welcome:

Śrī Narasingha Caitanya Maṭha
P.O. Box 21, Śrī Rangapatna
Karnataka - 571 438, India

— or —

Śrī Gaura-Gadādhāra Aśrama
RR-1, Box 300, W. Pawlet
Vermont 05775, U.S.A.

e-mail: gosai@gosai.com
web sites:
http://www.gosai.com/chaitanya
http://www.gosai.com/chaitanya/saranagati

Editor in Chief:
Tridaṇḍī Goswāmī Śrī Śrīmad
Bhakti Gaurava Narasingha Mahārāja

Associate Editors:
Śrīpāda Bhaktibhāvana Viṣṇu Mahārāja
Śrīpāda Bhaktivedānta Sajjana Mahārāja

Assisted by
numerous ever–aspiring servants
of Śrī Śrī Guru and Gaurāṅga

First printing:
1993 limited edition 1,000 copies

Second printing:
1998 limited edition 2,000 copies

Printed by
Srinivas Fine Arts (P) Ltd.
Bangalore, India
for the
International Gauḍīya
Vaiṣṇava Society

Dedicated To Our

Divine Spiritual Master

Viśvācārya Nitya-līlā-praviṣṭa

Oṁ Viṣṇupāda Paramahaṁsa

Parama Parivrājakācārya-varya

Aṣṭottara-śata Śrī Śrīmad Śrīla

A. C. Bhaktivedānta Swāmī

Prabhupāda

Contents

About the Author

HIS DIVINE GRACE A. C. Bhaktivedānta Swāmī Prabhupāda was a *rasika ācārya,* an expert in relishing the mellows of pure devotion as taught by Śrī Caitanya Mahāprabhu. Such capacity to relish hearing and chanting about Godhead's transcendental name, form, attributes, and pastimes is uncommon. The great *Śrīmad-Bhāgavatam* (6.14.5) informs us:

muktānām api siddhānāṁ
nārāyaṇa-parāyaṇaḥ
sudurlabaḥ praśāntātmā
koṭiṣv api mahā-mune

"Out of thousands of perfected souls, it is very rare to find one that is a pure devotee of God."

Perfection, or self-realization, is indeed a noteworthy accomplishment, yet it pales in comparison to unalloyed devotion. One need not fully surrender to God to achieve liberation from the flawed existence of material life. Any number of techniques may be employed in this attempt, but absolute humility of heart is not a requirement. Pure devotion, on the other hand, acknowledges no technique, while humility and absolute surrender are the stage on which the drama of divine love is eternally performed. His Divine Grace had such humility, such surrender, although he was at the same time often very demanding, insisting on a high standard from his disciples. Yet his assertiveness was all on behalf of Godhead and therefore justified. His assertiveness was an example of the dynamic face of humility, not an abstract, sterile humility, but the concrete and productive humility of doing God's bidding.

Śrīla Prabhupāda came to America in 1965 as "an aggressor." Aggression against illusion is the highest service to humanity. The cost of this war is absolute humility, for souls in this world are often less than thankful, unaware as they are of their own self-interest. The reward, however, is great. It is the dignity of the soul. This was the work of His Divine Grace: to bring dignity to all souls, and he did so with all of the humility at his command. It has been said that what Mohammed did with the sword, what Christianity did with wealth, he did with a humble heart—inundating the entire planet with love of God. The day will come when all men, women, and children from all races, countries, and creeds sing his praise.

For twelve years, beginning in 1965 until he disappeared from mortal vision in 1977, His Divine Grace circled the globe transplanting what was thought by many to be an Indian religion onto foreign soil. He demonstrated practically that Gauḍīya Vaiṣṇavism is not a product of a particular culture, but the *dharma* of the soul. He took the living conception of what he called Kṛṣṇa consciousness and extended its life beyond what the greatest Gauḍīya thinkers and practitioners of the time imagined was even remotely possible. Deep realization lies within the ability to adapt the spiritual reality to diverse material circumstances, making it accessible to one and all. This is the work of an *ācārya,* who teaches both by precept and example. The *ācārya* is not frozen in time. He is melted in love of Godhead, and flows without restriction to anyone and everyone who shows even the slightest interest in pure devotion. This was the work of His Divine Grace. He left a legacy of love, not law, for any and all of his immediate followers to embrace and continue. He gave to all, and looked for one—one who could actually understand his message.

Who was His Divine Grace? Founder *ācārya* of the International Society for Kṛṣṇa Consciousness, father, friend, and *śaktyaveśa avatāra* (empowered incarnation of a particular potency of God). *Nityānandaveśa,* the empowerment of Śrīpād Nityānanda Prabhu, the Lord Himself in His most merciful disposition, can only describe what we could see of Him with the outer eye attuned to the spiritual mind. The inner truth of Śrīla Prabhupāda's eternal form and personality will forever remain concealed to those who fail to embrace not merely the form, but the substance of all that he taught and all that he exemplified. The *darśana* (spiritual revelation) of his inner identity is his prerogative. May His Divine Grace mercifully bestow that most precious vision upon all who read this book.

Swāmī B.V. Tripurāri

Introduction

IN SEARCH OF THE ULTIMATE GOAL OF LIFE was written by our Divine Guide and Master, Oṁ Viṣṇupāda Paramahaṁsa Parivrājakācārya Aṣṭottara-śata Śrī Śrīmad A. C. Bhaktivedānta Swāmī Prabhupāda just after his entering the renounced order of life in the autumn of 1959. At that time, Śrīla Prabhupāda was living in Śrī Vṛndāvana-dhāma and would sometimes practice *mādhukarī*. *Mādhukarī* means to collect a little food door to door for one's maintenance just as the bee collects a little pollen flower to flower. Śrīla Prabhupāda, however, often requested the householders whom he called upon to give pen and paper for his writing rather than the rice, dahl, and chapatis traditionally sought by holy men practicing *mādhukarī*.

On those papers that he received as alms, Śrīla Prabhupāda wrote page after page, preparing his messages of Godhead for the world. Some of the manuscripts he published in his *Back to Godhead* magazine, and others, like *Easy Journey to Other Planets,* he printed as small booklets. Although unable to publish everything he wrote, Śrīla Prabhupāda nevertheless continued to write and stockpile his manuscripts. Unfortunately, some of the early writings of His Divine Grace were lost after Śrīla Prabhupāda left Śrī Vṛndāvana-dhāma to conduct his worldwide campaign of spreading Kṛṣṇa consciousness.

In 1977, just on the eve of our Divine Master's departure for the eternal abode of Śrī Śrī Rādhā-Kṛṣṇa, I found a handwritten manuscript at the bottom of an old metal trunk in the Rādhā-Dāmodara temple. The handwriting was easily recognizable as Śrīla Prabhupāda's. After the disappearance of His Divine Grace, I carried the manuscript with me wherever I went, showing it to interested devotees. On several occasions, my godbrothers suggested that I publish the manuscript for wide-scale distribution.

The original manuscript of more than two hundred pages was entitled *Lord Caitanya: His Sannyāsa and Saṅkīrtana Movement.* Unfortunately, 40 pages were missing from the middle section. For several years, we searched for those missing pages but were unable to find them. The manuscript was therefore divided into two parts. The first part describes Lord Caitanya's traveling from Navadvīpa-dhāma to Jagannātha Purī immediately after His accepting the *sannyāsa* order, the Lord's visiting the temple of Kṣiracorā Gopīnātha, the pastime of the Gopīnātha Deity stealing the offering of condensed milk to satisfy His pure devotee Śrīpād Mādhavendra Purī, and the pastime of the Śakṣi Gopāla Deity appearing as a witness to defeat the atheists. The second part of the manuscript describes the talks between Lord Caitanya and Rāmānanda Rāya when the two met on the banks of the river Godāvarī in South India.

In the second part of the manuscript, Śrīla Prabhupāda preaches very enthusiastically—discussing the *varṇāśrama* system, chastising the materialists, condemning the impersonalist conception, exposing the imitationists, praising the virtues and characteristics of pure devotion, and entering into confidential descriptions of the nature of *rāsā-tattva,* the transcendental mellowness of spontaneous love of Godhead.

Because the talks between Lord Caitanya and Rāmānanda Rāya had already been published by His Divine Grace in *The Teachings of Lord Caitanya* and his *Caitanya-caritāmṛta* purports, we hesitated to publish the manuscript, thinking that Śrīla Prabhupāda had already published what he wanted to say on the subject. However, by the grace of Śrīla Prabhupāda, I was inspired to read the manuscript again and again until finally I realized that my beloved *gurudeva* had expanded on some very confidential points in his original manuscript, which he did not fully reveal in either *The Teachings of Lord Caitanya* or the *Caitanya-caritāmṛta* purports.

The style of Śrīla Prabhupāda's writing in the manuscript is revealing. His Divine Grace makes his reader feel the urgency of Kṛṣṇa consciousness, a remarkable ability, which so much characterized his eminent position as a world *ācārya*. Taking his readers to the realm of divine love, Śrīla Prabhupāda extensively and freely reveals *mādhurya-premā*—the amorous love affairs of Śrīmatī Rādhārāṇī and Her cowherd girlfriends with Śrī Kṛṣṇa, the absolute King of Love, in the groves of Vṛndāvana—as the topmost platform of spontaneous love of Godhead. Thus the manuscript not only illuminates Śrīla Prabhupāda's position as a world *ācārya,* but reveals his position as an intimate associate of both Lord Caitanya Mahāprabhu and Śrī Śrī Rādhā-Kṛṣṇa. Therefore, although I am a most fallen soul, I still felt strongly that it would greatly please Śrīla Prabhupāda if I were to publish the second part of the manuscript under a separate title, which he himself uses in the manuscript: *In Search of the Ultimate Goal of Life.*

The talks between Lord Caitanya and Rāmānanda Rāya constitute the acme of all theistic conceptions, and thus are held in the highest regard by all Gauḍīya Vaiṣṇava *ācāryas.* The conversation between Lord Caitanya and Rāmānanda Rāya reveals the most esoteric truth about Vaiṣṇava philosophy, allowing the reader to enter into the inner identity of the Lord and the purpose of His appearance. These talks are an important topic of Gauḍīya Vaiṣṇava *siddhānta* for all aspiring devotees. Śrīla Prabhupāda's writing on this topic just after his accepting *sannyāsa* is evidence of the special importance of these discussions for people in the renounced order of life. That he did not venture to publish it immediately is further evidence of the highly confidential and esoteric nature of this essay.

Because the topic is a highly confidential subject matter, one may ask, "What is the need to publish it, thus making it available to even neophyte devotees?" The answer is that although Lord Caitanya Mahāprabhu requested that Rāmānanda Rāya not disclose this topic but keep it a secret, Śrīla Kṛṣṇadāsa Kavirāja Goswāmī in his *Caitanya-caritāmṛta* openly reveals the details of the Lord's talks with Rāmānanda and encourages all the devotees to enter deeply into their inner meaning.

Śrīla Prabhupāda calls the discussions between Lord Caitanya and Rāmānanda Rāya "In Search of the Ultimate Goal of Life" and requests his readers to enter into the essence of transcendental romance and pure love of Godhead by sincerely hearing his humble narration. Therefore, we felt that if we did not publish this manuscript, the worldwide community of devotees would be deprived of a most valuable gift.

As far as possible, we have tried to present the words of His Divine Grace in such a way as to preserve the original, charming mood of the author, but the readers must take into account that at the time of writing his manuscript Śrīla Prabhupāda had very little formal training in English or extensive contact with English-speaking people. Actually, His Divine Grace has simply allowed the editors of this book to render some menial service to his lotus feet out of his unlimited mercy, so we earnestly request that the readers try to grasp the spirit of this book and kindly forgive any defects there may be in our attempt to present it.

The devotees who have surrendered at the lotus feet of Lord Caitanya Mahāprabhu and desire only to become the servants of the maidservants of Śrī Śrī Rādhā-Kṛṣṇa will surely become enlivened by this publication. Others, who are not in the line of pure devotion, *rūpānuga-bhajana,* will not be able to understand the contents or the importance of this book. We humbly pray for the mercy of our Divine Master and for the blessings of all the Vaiṣṇavas that we may always be engaged in the heartfelt service of Lord Caitanya Mahāprabhu and His confidential associates as our life and soul.

Swāmī B.G. Narasingha

Praṇāmas by the Author

First of all, I beg to submit
to the lotus feet of my spiritual master,
Oṁ Viṣṇu-pāda Śrī Śrīmad Bhaktisiddhānta
Saraswatī Goswāmī Mahārāja,
who has opened my spiritual vision
and eradicated the darkness of ignorance
by his forceful message of the transcendental world.
It is only by the mercy of His Divine Grace
that I have been able to remove
the impersonal calamity.

I offer my most sincere obeisances
unto the lotus feet of the Lord of Lords,
who is the protector of all surrendered souls.
The Supreme Lord is always anxious to bestow
upon us the fortune of unalloyed love of God,
untouched by such deviating processes
as dry speculative empiric knowledge
or the unsatiated desire for fruitive activities
meant only to acquire temporary material gains.
He is the supreme leader of the chain of disciplic succession
in the line of Śrīla Ānanda Tīrtha.
He is worshiped by Śrī Śrīman Adwaita Prabhu
and Śrī Śrīman Haridāsa Ṭhākura,
who are incarnations of Mahā-Viṣṇu
and Brahmā respectively.
He delivers His devotees, such as
the brāhmaṇa leper Vāsudeva,
from all ailments.

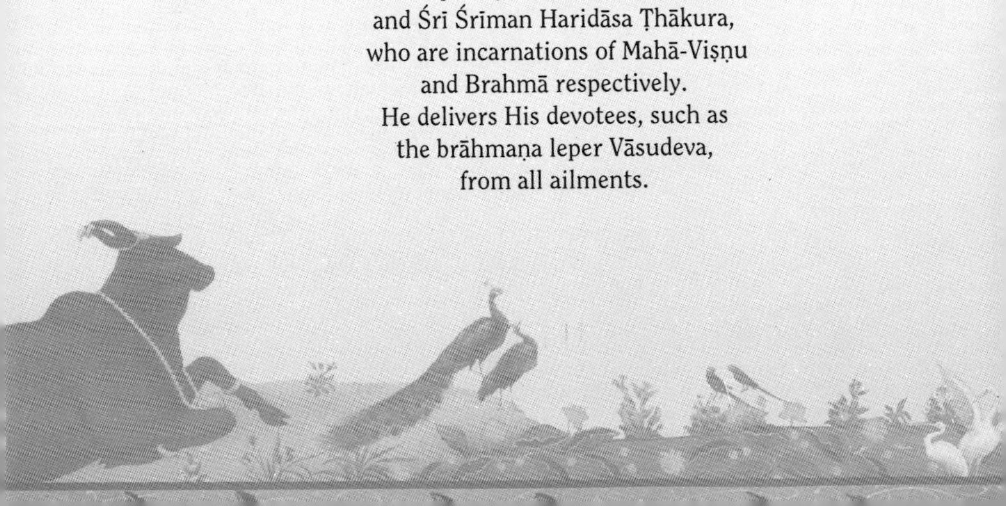

He is the deliverer
of Sārvabhauma Bhaṭṭācārya
and King Pratāparudra,
who were suffering from the pangs
of material renunciation
and enjoyment respectively.

I offer my most sincere obeisances
unto the lotus feet of the Lord of Lords
who superficially accepted
the renounced life of a sannyāsī
to make the brāhmaṇa's curse effective.
In the garb of a sannyāsī, He initiated
the transcendental ecstasy of spontaneous love of God
as was felt by Śrīmatī Rādhārāṇī
in Her amorous desire to meet Śrī Kṛṣṇa.
In the quest of such spontaneous love of God,
the Lord relinquished the association
of His eternal consort Śrī Lakṣmī Viṣṇupriyā Devī,
who was dearest to Him and whose mercy is most ardently
sought after by all true devotees of God
and even by the denizens of heaven.
The Lord accepted the renounced order of life
in accordance with the foretelling inculcated
in the Mahābhārata, the Vedas, and the Śrīmad Bhāgavatam
in order to bestow His causeless mercy upon us,
who are addicted to the false enjoyment of
fame, glory, the opposite sex, and wealth
in this material world.

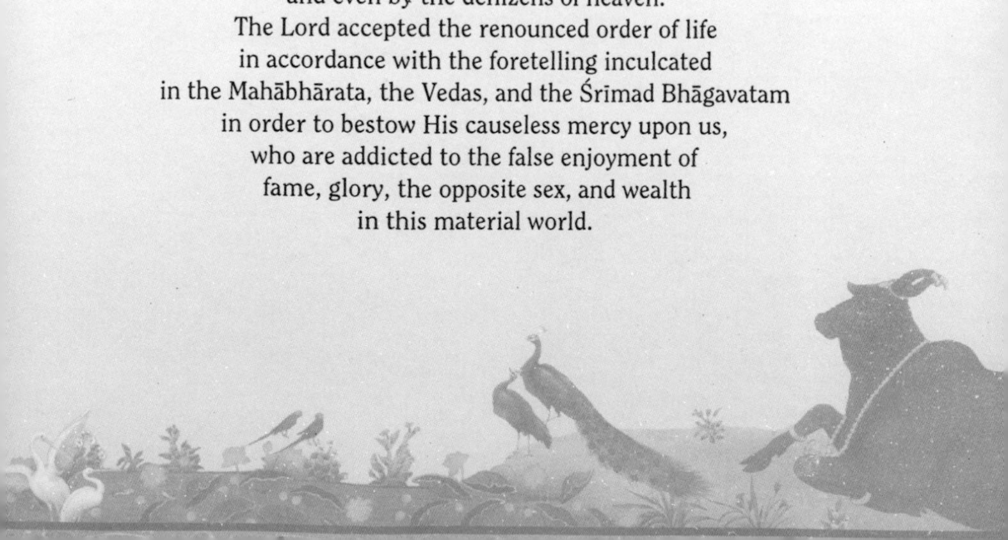

WHILE ON TOUR of South India, Lord Caitanya Mahāprabhu arrived on the banks of the river Godāvarī, where He met Śrī Rāmānanda Rāya, a great devotee of Śrī Kṛṣṇa. Lord Caitanya expressed a deep desire to hear about Śrī Kṛṣṇa from the lips of Rāmānanda Rāya and requested that Rāmānanda recite a verse from the revealed scriptures concerning the ultimate goal of life. Rāmānanda then replied:

sva-dharmācaraṇe viṣṇu-bhakti haya

"If a person performs the prescribed duties of his social position, he awakens his original Kṛṣṇa consciousness."

Supporting his statement, Rāmānanda then cited a verse from the *Viṣṇu Purāṇa* (3.8.9):

varṇāśramācāravatā
puruṣeṇa paraḥ pumān
viṣṇur ārādhyate panthā
nānyat tat-doṣa-kāraṇam

"The Personality of Godhead Lord Viṣṇu is worshiped by the proper performance of prescribed duties in the system of *varṇa* and *āśrama*. There is no other way to satisfy the Personality of Godhead. One must be situated in the institution of the four *varṇas* and *āśramas*."

Varṇa and Āśrama Jeopardized

Hearing this statement from Rāmānanda Rāya, Lord Caitanya replied that the system of *varṇāśrama-dharma* was external and thus it was not acceptable. Lord Caitanya also rejected the statement of Rāmānanda because the system of *varṇāśrama-dharma* is now jeopardized by the influence of the present age of Kali, the age of quarrel and fighting.

In the *Bhāgavad-gītā,* the Personality of Godhead declares that the *varṇāśrama* system is created by Him, although He is aloof from such a system. Because the *varṇāśrama* system is a creation of the Personality of Godhead, it is not possible to do away with it. However, the nefarious activities of the people of the age of Kali can jeopardize the *varṇāśrama* system. We have purposely used the word *jeopardized* because the whole system still exists but in a reflected form.

In the *varṇāśrama* system of social management, the aim of life is to attain the favor of Lord Viṣṇu, the all-pervading Personality of Godhead. Unfortunately, at the present moment the aim of life is to displease the all-pervading Godhead and thereby suffer perpetually under the laws of material nature. The goal of the *varṇāśrama* system is to peacefully perform the prescribed duties of humanity and thereby achieve the highest success, namely the favor of Lord Viṣṇu. But when the aim of life is the planned exploitation of material nature, all life is jeopardized on account of the human race fighting with the laws of nature.

The arrangement of nature is so strict that even a slight violation of the laws of nature can do great harm to a conditioned human being. Human beings must always consider themselves to be living under the stringent laws of nature. They must always remember that their plans for breaking nature's laws will bring about tremendous hardship. Regrettably, human beings under the deluding influence of material nature want to lord it over the laws of nature, and, as such, they are more and more entangled in conditioned life. Foolish human beings do not see the defect of their so-called advancement of knowledge. The most difficult problems of life are birth, death, old age, and disease. These four problems are a permanent settlement for the conditioned soul. Human beings want to lord it over the laws of nature but their so-called advancement of scientific knowledge cannot solve these problems.

A continuous increase of world population to the proportion of three births in every second has puzzled the brains of the leaders of society. To solve the problem of birth, they put forward rascal plans of birth control under the name of family planning, yet the problem is unsolved. By the laws of nature, the population is ever-increasing in spite of all their scientific plans and schemes. On the whole, the problem of birth has remained unsolved.

Mother Nature's Atom Bomb

The death problem is also not solved. None of the scientific knowledge of the human being has solved the death problem. The advancement of material knowledge can simply accelerate the problem of dying; nobody can save a person from the cruel hands of death. The discovery of the atom bomb and similar other great inventions of the fertile brain of the scientist has simply increased the death problem. The foolish scientists do not know that the atom bomb is actually the scheme of Mother Nature, who is sure to kill the demoniac population when it increases disproportionately.

Modern economists also believe in the laws of nature and confirm that unrestricted birth increases in the human population will certainly result in famine, pestilence, epidemics, and war. So, the so-called civilized states' plan of killing human beings by atomic and hydrogen bombs is actually the plan of Mother Nature to punish the foolish miscreants.

Everything is automatically executed by Mother Nature as soon as the human being is in violation of her laws. However, foolish people, out of their undue vanity, think that the plan is made by them. To execute her stringent punishment, Mother Nature dictates to the human brain the ability to invent the atomic bomb. Foolishly, the human being wants to take the credit for such inventions, which are meant only for punishment. We learn this fact from the *Bhāgavad-gītā* (3.27), wherein it is said that everything is done by *prakṛti* or Mother Nature. But the foolish living entity, puffed up by the vanity of learning, falsely considers himself the Creator.

The Problem Remains the Same

Without going further into the details of birth and death in terms of modernized scientific plans, it can safely be said that the problem of birth and death remains in its original proportion. Nothing has been done to increase or decrease the problem.

The problem of old age and disease is also not solved. The more the inventions of modernized science are made, the more relative diseases increase proportionately.

We can again conclude that birth, death, old age, and disease are the sum total of all the problems of material existence and can never be solved by any plan made by human beings. If a human being wants to solve all the problems of material existence, he must abide by the advice of Godhead that only by full surrender unto Him can one be saved from the stringent conditions of the material laws of nature.

Perverted Castes

The system of *varṇāśrama-dharma* as it is mentioned in the scriptures aims at achieving the favor of Lord Viṣṇu. This is the only solution to the problem of birth and death. The jeopardized system of *varṇāśrama-dharma* has produced a perverted form, commonly known as the caste system. The caste system is now represented by the political diplomats, the soldiers, the capitalists, and the laborers. The politicians or the best planning brains of the human race have taken the position of *brāhmaṇas*. Surely the *brāhmaṇa* possesses the best brain for solving the problems of human life, but the politicians are simply using the best part of their brains for executing their own selfish plans. Avoiding the orders of the Supreme Godhead, they only bring disorder to the society.

The military arrangement is a false representation of the *kṣatriyas*, who are meant to give protection to the public at large. However, the military leaders of every country are sucking the blood of the masses by imposing heavy, unbearable taxes, instead of giving any actual protection.

The capitalists, who represent *vaiśyas*, instead of accumulating wealth for carrying out the will of Lord Viṣṇu, are amassing huge wealth for their own sense gratification. As a result of this, many problems, such as political policies that exploit the masses, have sprung up in all parts of the world. The laborers are a perverted representation of the *śūdras*, who are serving the capitalists under the pressure of many obligations. They are always groaning to make an adjustment to the labor problem by raising political issues.

The system of *varṇāśrama-dharma* has not been ostracized as some may wish, but the whole system has now been pervertedly represented by politicians in the position of *brāhmaṇas*; military men in the position of the *kṣatriyas*; individual capitalists in the position of the *vaiśyas*; and the ordinary laborers in the position of the *śūdras*. The whole system is perverted by the lawbreaking attitude of mankind. This is spoiling the atmosphere of peaceful progress in human life. At present, the system of perverted *varṇāśrama-dharma* cannot in any way please the Supreme Godhead Viṣṇu. Thus no one can escape the police action of Mother Nature, regardless of how expert one may be in material science.

Real Varṇa and Āśrama

The *varṇāśrama* system, originated by the Personality of Godhead, is spiritually significant because when all the *varṇas* and *āśramas* cooperate, society facilitates deliverance from the clutches of *māyā* or illusion. This is done by all *varṇas* and *āśramas* carrying out the plan of Godhead. The *brāhmaṇa* is considered the mouth of the *virāṭ-puruṣa* (the cosmophysical feature of the Personality of Godhead). The *kṣatriyas* are the arms, the *vaiśyas* are the stomach, and the *śūdras* are the legs. The functioning of the mouth is recognized by sound. Therefore, the function of the *brāhmaṇas* or *sannyāsīs* is to transmit the transcendental sound of the *Vedas* so that every human being can know what is what in relation to the Supreme. By transmission of transcendental sound, human beings will know their actual identities as superior in nature to matter. Thus they will know their eternal relationship with Godhead. Knowing this, they will be engaged in carrying out the plan of Godhead, instead of serving the deluding energy with a false notion of lording it over her. Carrying out the plan of Godhead will help the conditioned soul get out of the clutches of the deluding energy and enter into the kingdom of God for an eternal life of bliss and knowledge.

Every living being is struggling in this material world for eternal life, knowledge, and bliss, but is bewildered by the deluding energy. The plan of Godhead is so designed that in the human form of life one can get out of the entanglement of material existence. Because the *kṣatriyas* are the arms of the *virāṭ-puruṣa,* it is their duty to protect the whole body and cooperate with the mouth, stomach, and legs. The system of *varṇāśrama* is a spiritual plan of cooperation for mutual benefit, and therefore it is essential that it be maintained in its original dignity. As it stands now, it is perverted and diseased.

The so-called *brāhmaṇas* have become detached from the body of the *virāṭ-puruṣa* because they do not transmit the transcendental sounds of the *Vedas*. A head that is cut off from the body certainly cannot produce any sound. Such a dead head, although called a *brāhmaṇa,* has no real value as a head. Similarly, those *brāhmaṇas* who simply claim to be so by a custom of hereditary right also have no value as *brāhmaṇas,* because they have no power to function as the mouth of Godhead. In the same manner, whoever fails to carry out the plan of Godhead as part and parcel of the *virāṭ-puruṣa* must be considered fallen and detached from his position. Such separated parts are of no value as mouths, arms, stomachs, or legs.

Varṇa and Āśrama Rejected

Thus Lord Caitanya rejected Rāmānanda's proposal, because in the age of Kali the *varṇāśrama-dharma* is so degraded that any attempt to restore it to its original position will be hopeless. He also rejected *varṇāśrama-dharma* because it has no value in relation to pure devotional service.

The second, more important consideration is that even if the *varṇāśrama* system is observed strictly, it still cannot help one to rise to the highest plane of transcendental service to Godhead. The *virāṭ-puruṣa* is a material conception of the Personality of Godhead and is just the beginning of spiritual realization. The topmost spiritual realization is attraction for devotional service to the Personality of Godhead. Such attraction for devotional service is the only necessity for the living being and it automatically brings a sense of detachment from all other activities.

The Personality of Godhead is worshiped by pure devotional service and He becomes available to His devotees through such devotion. Pure devotional service is produced by cultivation of pure knowledge and activities under the regulative principles of the scriptures. Thus the *varṇāśrama* system is explained in relation to pure devotion by Bhagavān Puruṣa, the Personality of Godhead Śrī Kṛṣṇa, who descended to this material world for the deliverance of all fallen souls. The *Bhāgavad-gītā* (18.45-46) states:

sve sve karmaṇy abhirataḥ
saṁsiddhiṁ labhate naraḥ
sva-karma-nirataḥ siddhiṁ
yathā vindati tac chṛṇu

yataḥ pravṛttir bhūtānāṁ
yena sarvam idaṁ tatam
sva-karmaṇā tam abhyarcya
siddhiṁ vindati mānavaḥ

"Every human being will attain the highest goal of life simply by worshiping the Personality of Godhead, from whom all the living entities have come into being and by whom the whole cosmos is generated and again withdrawn."

Worshiping Godhead by prescribed duties is the beginning of devotional service, and all the great sages like Taṅka, Dramiḍa, Bhāruci, Bodhāyana, Guhadeva, and Kapardi have approved of this system of gradual progress. All the ancient authorities have commented upon the *Vedas* in accordance with this principle. The authorities of the Rāmānuja sect of Vaiṣṇavas also affirm the above:

> The easiest way of attaining the Absolute Truth is to culture knowledge about the Absolute Truth as it is described in the scriptures while simultaneously performing one's prescribed duty. This process is almost direct realization of the path of devotional service. Realization of the Absolute Truth by proper observance of the *varṇāśrama* system does not mean to accept only the renounced order of life *sannyāsa*, but it means that everyone can attain the highest goal by the performance of his own duties. Proper performance does not necessarily mean to take *sannyāsa*.

Rāmānanda Rāya, after being asked by Lord Caitanya to define the highest standard of perfection in human life, had taken up the cause of ordinary people and supported the utility of *varṇāśrama-dharma* by quoting the *Viṣṇu Purāṇa*. He said that the performance of duties according to *varṇāśrama-dharma* should be taken as the highest perfection of life.

Yet because the *varṇāśrama-dharma* system is a problem within the material world in the age of Kali, Lord Caitanya wanted to distinguish it from the devotional activities, which are transcendental by nature. Taking into consideration the transcendental nature of devotional service, which is the highest perfection of life, Lord Caitanya declared the system of *varṇāśrama-dharma* to be external. Lord Caitanya wanted human beings to make further advancement in the process of spiritual realization than what is possible by the performance of *varṇāśrama-dharma*.

Although the aim of *varṇāśrama-dharma* is to satisfy the all-pervading Godhead Viṣṇu, it does not explicitly mention devotional service rendered directly to the Personality of Godhead. Without being specifically engaged in devotional service, even the proper performance of *varṇāśrama-dharma* may lead one to accept either the impersonal or personal feature of Godhead. Impersonal realization of the Absolute Truth will mar the progress of devotional service. Therefore, Lord Caitanya did not wish to risk the human life in that way, and thus He rejected *varṇāśrama-dharma* as external.

Lord Caitanya's rejection of the value of *varṇāśrama-dharma* indicated that Rāmānanda should suggest a more comprehensive process of self-realization.

Hodge-podge Impersonalism

Taking the hint from Lord Caitanya, Rāmānanda Rāya quoted a verse from the *Bhāgavad-gītā* (9.27) about the process of dedicating all one's *karma* (fruitive actions) to Śrī Kṛṣṇa, the Personality of Godhead.

yat karoṣi yad aśnāsi
yaj juhoṣi dadāsi yat
yat tapasyasi kaunteya
yat kuruṣva mad-arpaṇam

"O son of Kuntī, all that you do, all that you eat, all that you offer or give away, as well as all austerities that you perform, do as an offering unto Me."

To give and take means one *person* giving and another *person* receiving. This distinct feature of dealings between the living entity and the Personality of Godhead is a more clear conception of ones proper relationship with the Absolute Truth than that which is found in *varṇāśrama-dharma*.

The present age of Kali is almost fully surcharged with the imperfect idea of the Absolute Truth being impersonal. The *māyāvāda* school has chiefly fathered this impersonal idea of the Absolute Truth by systematic propaganda since the time of Śrīpād Śaṅkarācārya. People of demoniac nature, who are now flourishing in all parts of the world, have relished this hodge-podge impersonal idea of the Absolute Truth for their own less than spiritual purposes.

The materialistic people of the world are practically all atheistic and immoral due to the infectious conditions of Kali-yuga. The Kali-yuga is predominated by illegitimate connection with the opposite sex, killing of animals, intoxication, and gambling. The materialists are almost all notorious for all these kinds of nefarious works in spite of their so-called education and knowledge. They are, in the language of the *Bhāgavad-gītā, duṣkṛtina,* qualified in the wrong way. When a human being's activity is targeted towards self-realization, it is right activity. Wrong activity means entangling oneself more and more in the conditions of material nature. *Kṛti* means one who is qualified and *duṣ* means the wrong way. So the combined word *duṣkṛtina* means one who is qualified in the wrong way.

Educated Means Atheist

The advancement of material education has produced many graduates, postgraduates, professors, and many other so-called enlightened people in this age of Kali, but most of them are being wrongly educated. The result is that the more people are educated, the more they become immoral and atheistic. Moreover, wrongly educated people have practically no faith in the scriptural injunctions. They have no respect for the self-realized sages who have left behind many valuable literary works, which are considered the treasure chest of spiritual cultivation.

To further misguide these wrongly qualified persons, the *pāṣaṇḍīs* or atheists in the garb of spiritual instructors encourage them in the wrong method of livelihood. This has been predicted in the *Śrīmad-Bhāgavatam* (12.4.43-44). Śukadeva Goswāmī addressed King Parīkṣit, "O my King, in the age of Kali, almost all the people who are destined to die do not worship the Absolute Personality of Godhead who is the Lord of the universe and is respectfully obeyed by all the demigods such as Brahmā, Mahādeva, Indra, and others. Unfortunately, the people in the age of Kali worship *pāṣaṇḍīs*, who misrepresent the teachings of the *Vedas* by atheistic culture. These people, infected by the sinful activities of Kali, do not worship the Personality of Godhead, the remembrance of whose name only—even by a dying person, a person in trouble, or a person who has fallen down—can deliver all from distress and sin, and lift them to the highest goal of life."

The *pāṣaṇḍīs* have most successfully misdirected the so-called enlightened people of Kali-yuga. They have successfully produced or manufactured many *avatāras* or incarnations of Godhead of their own choice without any reference to the *śāstras* (scriptures) and propagated the false idea of impersonal liberation as the highest achievement in life.

Śaṅkara Astonished

These impersonalists of the present age declare themselves to be the followers of Śrīpād Śaṅkarācārya, but even if Śaṅkarācārya himself happened to appear, he would be astonished to see his so-called followers. In fact, these impersonalists are all atheists and materialists. They have nothing to do either with the actual *brahmavāda* school of Śaṅkarācārya or with the *bhāgavata sampradāya* represented by the Vaiṣṇava *ācāryas.*

The impersonal conception of the Absolute Truth, as propounded by the so-called *brahmavāda* school, falls short of spiritual progress from its first step. Śaṅkarācārya's impersonal conception of *brahmavāda* had some meaning because he emphasized renouncing material activities. His ideal example of renunciation, as personally practiced and taught by him, has great significance for the demoniac people of the age of Kali, but the present impersonalists do not follow Śaṅkarācārya or the *śāstra.* They do, however, preach something that is not only absurd from all spiritual points of view, but is the start of material enjoyment, which they try to cover with the red garments of renunciation. These so-called followers of Śrīpād Śaṅkarācārya are condemned by Śaṅkarācārya himself, because they have taken the red dress simply for the matter of filling their bellies.

The atheistic impersonalists have done tremendous harm to the potential for spiritual advancement of the people in general. Therefore, the impersonalists have become the principal target of reformation for the peaceful *saṅkīrtana* movement of Lord Caitanya.

Absolute Truth is Personal

The Absolute Truth is ultimately a person who is supreme and all-powerful. He is called Puruṣottama. Impersonal *Brahman* is the effulgence of His personal body and localized Paramātmā or the Supersoul is His plenary part. That is the verdict of all the *śāstras,* especially the *Bhagavad-gītā, Śrīmad-Bhāgavatam,* and all other allied transcendental literatures. The whole *saṅkīrtana* movement of Lord Caitanya is aimed at giving importance to the Personality of Godhead and His transcendental service. As such, Lord Caitanya always regarded the impersonal conception of the Absolute Truth as detrimental to the path of devotional activities. He considered the system of *varṇāśrama-dharma* to be external because even if *varṇāśrama-dharma* is properly carried out, one still cannot get a clear conception of the Personality of Godhead.

Rāmānanda's suggestion of the *śloka* from the *Bhagavad-gītā* about offering everything to Kṛṣṇa definitely advances the conception of the Personality of Godhead, but still the practice of this conception is not fully transcendental. Thus the *varṇāśrama-dharma* conception can hardly help to raise the practitioner to the transcendental spiritual plane. Lord Caitanya thus rejected this material conception of the Personality of Godhead and called it external.

No Clear Idea

The grossly materialistic people cannot understand how it is possible to give away the result of one's own work. It is impossible for grossly materialistic people to part with their earnings that are made by their personal effort. Such gross materialists can simply get information from the suggestion that they have to give away the result of their personal labor to the Personality of Godhead. But because they do not have a clear idea of the Personality of Godhead or the process of giving the result of their earnings to the Personality of Godhead, it is very difficult for them to practice this conception.

When Lord Caitanya rejected Rāmānanda Rāya's second suggestion of directly offering the fruits of one's actions to God rather than indirectly through the *varṇāśrama* system, Rāmānanda then made a third suggestion. He proposed that ordinary people, who are fully engaged in the act of earning and enjoying, improve their life by giving up the process of continuing to live in the material world while offering the fruits of their labor to God. On the basis of this improved idea, Rāmānanda quoted a *śloka* from *Śrīmad-Bhāgavatam* (11.11.32):

ājñāyaivaṁ guṇān doṣān
mayādiṣṭān api svakān
dharmān saṁtyajya yaḥ sarvān
māṁ bhajet sa ca sattamaḥ

In this *śloka,* the Personality of Godhead says, "Occupational duties are described in the religious scriptures. If one analyzes them, one can fully understand their qualities and faults and then give them up completely to render service unto Me. Such a person is accepted as a saint of the highest order."

This conception is based on the fact that ultimately the acceptance of the devotional service of Godhead is the highest aim of religious perfection. By performing religious duties, if we can reach pure devotion, we may be considered first-class *sādhus* or saints.

Accept Sannyāsa

Rāmānanda suggested that we give up practicing the rules of *varṇāśrama-dharma* and take *sannyāsa*. Acceptance of *sannyāsa* means to renounce materialistic life, and in doing so one has to engage fully in the devotional service of Godhead. In support of this idea, Rāmānanda quoted the above *śloka* from the *Śrīmad-Bhāgavatam*. He also supported his suggestion with another *śloka* from the *Bhagavad-gītā* (18.66):

sarva-dharmān parityajya
mām ekaṁ śaraṇaṁ vraja
ahaṁ tvāṁ sarva-pāpebhyo
mokṣayiṣyāmi mā śucaḥ

Here, the Personality of Godhead desires that everyone give up all other religious considerations and engage wholly and solely in following Him exclusively. "I will protect you from all difficulties arising out of renouncing all other engagements. You have nothing to fear."

Go Higher

An improved consciousness for the materialists is a desire to either retire from material activities or stay at a place that is undisturbed by the uproar of the modes of nature. The river Virajā is outside the boundary of the material world where there is no disturbance from the three modes of nature. The material world is the creation of the external energy of Godhead, and Vaikuṇṭha, the spiritual world, is the creation of the internal energy of Godhead. Virajā is situated between the material world and the spiritual world. It is outside the boundary of both the material and the spiritual world. However, renunciation without any positive engagement is imperfect and cannot give the candidate the desired result of love of God.

The aim of Lord Caitanya is to bring people to the spiritual world. Therefore, this suggestion of Rāmānanda, which does not take one within the boundary of Vaikuṇṭha, was also rejected by the Lord. Negating the material activities or becoming disinterested in material activities does not suggest accepting positive spiritual activities. Spiritual activities completely depend on spiritual understanding. People having no realization of the spiritual world cannot sustain themselves by giving up all other activities. One must have a positive transcendental engagement. Otherwise, simply negating the material activities of religiosity will not help one the slightest bit in spiritual realization. By such renunciation, one will simply feed a void in his life and will again be attracted by the material activities for want of actual spiritual engagements. This sort of spiritual realization is another type of impersonal conception and is therefore not ultimately suitable for the prospective devotee.

Mixed Devotion

Rāmānanda, having realized the desire of Lord Caitanya, then suggested an improved process, called calculated devotion (*jñāna-miśra-bhakti*). Driven by a false sense of oneness with the Absolute Truth, the empiric philosopher tries to make an analytical study of the cosmic situation to find out the Absolute Truth. When he has done so, he becomes cheerful on account of his self-realization.

The symptoms of perfect realization of the Absolute Truth, which promote one to the stage of pure devotional service to the Personality of Godhead, are described in the *Bhagavad-gītā* (18.54). This was quoted by Rāmānanda as a further improvement on the suggestion of renunciation of *karma*:

brahma-bhūtaḥ prasannātmā
na śocati na kāṅkṣati
samaḥ sarveṣu bhūteṣu
mad-bhaktiṁ labhate parām

"The practitioner who has realized the Absolute Truth as the nondifferentiated impersonal *Brahman* does not lament over any material loss, neither does he desire any material gain. He is equipoised towards all objects of the material world, and these conditions make him fit to be promoted to the pure devotional service of Godhead."

However, the *brahma-bhūtaḥ* state of consciousness is also not a fully transcendental state of spiritual existence. The supramental consciousness, as exists in the spiritual kingdom of Vaikuṇṭha, is a further development. The *brahma-bhūtaḥ* state of consciousness is undoubtedly free from gross material consciousness, and although touching the Absolute Truth indicates a transcendental feeling, it is not the actual transcendental position for realizing the activities of Vaikuṇṭha. As such, it is also external.

Lord Caitanya wants the living entity to be free from every type of material consciousness, including becoming unconcerned with empiric knowledge and fruitive activities. One should stay in pure consciousness, as even a slight tinge of material consciousness causes an impersonal conception of the Absolute Truth. In all these different stages of material consciousness, only imaginary arguments predominate over the Absolute Personality of Godhead. Imaginary argumentative endeavors are detrimental to the pure devotional service of Godhead, and, as such, even the liberated state as above mentioned is external. This liberated state is something like the convalescent stage after relief from a disease. If a convalescent person is not properly taken care of, a relapse of the disease may mar the whole attempt at recovery.

In the *brahma-bhūta* liberated stage, one has not yet obtained a resting place at the lotus feet of the Personality of Godhead. As such, one is still unsupported and thus runs the chance of falling down again into material activities. It is therefore also external and thus the fourth suggestion of Rāmānanda was rejected by Lord Caitanya.

Knowledge-free Devotion

Rāmānanda then suggested the beginning of pure devotional service unconcerned with empiric knowledge or fruitive activity. To support this suggestion, Rāmānanda quoted a statement of Brahmā during his prayer of regret before Śrī Kṛṣṇa, the Personality of Godhead:

jñāne prayāsam udapāsya namanta eva
jīvanti san-mukharitāṁ bhavadīya-vārtām
stāne stitāḥ śruti-gatāṁ tanu-vāṅ-manobhir
ye prāyaśo 'jita jito 'py asi tais tri-lokyām

"O my Lord, those devotees who completely give up the attempt to become one with You by the culture of empiric knowledge and simply try to hear about Your glories from the mouths of self-realized saints, and who live a virtuous life, can easily achieve Your favor although You are unconquerable by anyone within the three worlds."(*Bhāg.* 10.14.3)

This stage of culturing devotional service directly was accepted by Lord Caitanya. All the previously described stages of the culture of spiritual realization were rejected by Lord Caitanya most logically. The Lord, however, accepted the universal method of hearing the glories of the Personality of Godhead in all circumstances from the mouths of self-realized souls and giving up the attempt to become one with Godhead.

The poison of attempting to become one with Godhead kills the nucleus of devotional service. Anyone actually desiring to be engaged in the transcendental loving service of Godhead must definitely give up this idea for good. In the *Caitanya-caritāmṛta,* it is said that the idea of being one with Godhead is the topmost type of pretension, and even a slight development of this idea will completely eliminate the prospect for devotional service. This is the most dangerous misconception in spiritual life and one should at once give up the idea.

Hear From Self-realized Souls

A pure living entity, being always subservient to the Almighty Godhead Śrī Kṛṣṇa, should reverentially give an aural reception to the transcendental sound emanating from the mouth of a self-realized soul describing the glories of the Personality of Godhead. Only a self-realized soul can produce the powerful effect of transcendental sound. Devotees must live thoroughly honest lives in all respects by their body, mind, and words. These are the simple methods of culturing spiritual realization to its zenith.

Lord Caitanya approved of this simple method for all classes of people without any distinction of caste, creed, color, or education. The only qualification of the practitioners that is essential for this spiritual culture is that they at once give up the idea of becoming one with Godhead. This idea of becoming one with Godhead is generally only acquired by the empiric philosopher, but otherwise every human being naturally feels that God is greater than himself and that he is always subservient to all His wishes. Even a great personality like Mahātmā Gandhi always spoke in terms of "God is great." Gandhi often said, "Not a blade of grass moves without the sanction of God."

Therefore, the imaginary idea of becoming one with Godhead is a mental creation of the empiric philosopher as a result of his material vanity. Otherwise, the idea has no substance. The idea of becoming one with Godhead is artificial and a simple-hearted person is always against such an idea. Rejecting the idea of becoming one with Godhead is always natural for everyone and nobody has to make any special attempt to dismiss this foolishness.

The next qualification is to become gentle and humble when hearing from a self-realized soul. The *Bhagavad-gītā* is the direct transcendental message of Godhead, and the prospective devotee must receive this message with all gentleness and humility from a self-realized soul.

The method of receiving the message of Godhead, as mentioned in the fourth chapter of the *Bhagavad-gītā,* is to hear from the chain of disciplic succession. It is said there that the system of spiritual realization was first disclosed to Vivasvān, the sun-god, who transmitted the message to Manu, the father of mankind. Manu then transmitted the subject to his son Ikṣvāku. By the transcendental method of disciplic succession, the system was realized by all the *rājarṣis,* saintly kings. Unfortunately, the chain was broken and the message had to again be revived beginning with Arjuna, the friend and devotee of Śrī Kṛṣṇa.

The prospective devotee's qualification of hearing the transcendental message will not depend on birth, heritage, education, caste, creed, color, or nationality, but will depend on humility and finding the proper source for receiving the transcendental message. The mystery of the message as mentioned in the *Bhagavad-gītā* must therefore be understood in terms of the realization of Arjuna and nobody else. The realization of Arjuna is also mentioned in the *Bhagavad-gītā*, and whoever speaks in the line of that realization is to be considered a self-realized soul. The message of *Bhagavad-gītā* is to be heard from a self-realized soul and not from anyone speculating on dry subjects with imaginary meanings. The un-bona-fide attempt at hearing will simply be a waste of time. The devotee must always be careful that the speaker is in the transcendental line of disciplic succession called the *paramparā.*

The qualification of the prospective devotee should be that he must live an honest life by his body, mind, and words, which will all depend on the mercy of Godhead.

Spontaneous Love of Godhead

Thus the preliminary stage of culturing devotional service without any touch of speculative knowledge was accepted by Lord Caitanya who then asked Rāmānanda Rāya to proceed further in developing the service sentiment to higher and higher stages of love of Godhead until the highest stage was reached. To this Rāmānanda answered that the progress in this line will end in the loving service of Godhead. Every living entity has within his heart a dormant and eternal love of Godhead. Spiritual culture is the attempt to revive that eternal love of Godhead to its spontanous stage, and the beginning of that attempt is receiving the transcendental message of Godhead from the right source—a self-realized soul. After receiving the transcendental message, this conception has to be developed to the spontaneous stage of love of Godhead. Rāmānanda describes the process in the following words:

nānopacāra-kṛta-pūjanam ārta-bandhoḥ
premṇaiva bhakta-hṛdayaṁ sukha-vidrutaṁ syāt
yāvat kṣud asti jaṭhare jaraṭhā pipāsā
tāvat sukhāya bhavato nanu bhakṣya-peye

"As long as there is acute hunger in the stomach, there is pleasure in eating and drinking. Similarly, as long as ecstatic spontaneous love of God is aroused in the mind of a devotee, the worship of Godhead with all kinds of paraphernalia becomes the real cause of happiness." (*Padyāvalī* 13)

The purport of this statement is that hunger is the cause of pleasure in taking foodstuffs. Similarly, spontaneous love of Godhead is the cause of all pleasure in spiritual culture.

Śrī Rāmānanda Rāya quoted another *śloka* as follows:

kṛṣṇa-bhakti-rasa-bhāvitā matiḥ
krīyatāṁ yadi kuto 'pi labhyate
tatra laulyam api mūlyam ekalaṁ
janma-koṭi-sukṛtair na labhyate

"The intelligence for achieving the loving service of Godhead may be purchased from anywhere it is available. The price for such a purchase is a strong desire for achieving such a stage of life. Such a strong desire for rendering loving service unto the Personality of Godhead is very, very rare because it is developed by accumulating the results of many virtuous purifying acts in thousands and thousands of lives." (*Padyāvalī* 14)

The desire for rendering loving service unto the Personality of Godhead is an invaluable desire and it brings the highest spiritual perfection. It is very rarely seen in the ordinary course of life. Lord Caitanya, being the most magnanimous incarnation of the Personality of Godhead, out of His kindness and causeless mercy upon the fallen souls of this age of Kali, is prepared to bestow the highest benefit of life by the simple method of hearing and chanting the glories of the Personality of Godhead. This is the beginning of the transcendental method, gradually reaching to the stage of spontaneous love of Godhead.

Dāsya-Premā

To develop the conception, Lord Caitanya asked Rāmānanda to go further. As such, Rāmānanda first suggested the devotional service called *dāsya-premā* or the mellow of transcendental servitude. He quoted a verse from *Śrīmad-Bhāgavatam* that was uttered by Durvāsā Muni. Durvāsā Muni, with the pride of a caste *brāhmaṇa,* envied the pure devotee Mahārāja Ambarīṣa, who happened to be a householder king and by caste a *kṣatriya*. Durvāsā Muni wanted to put Mahārāja Ambarīṣa in trouble by the strength of his mystic prowess.

When Ambarīṣa Mahārāja was put into trouble, the disc weapon of Lord Viṣṇu, *sudarśana cakra,* appeared to rescue Mahārāja Ambarīṣa and attack Durvāsā for his nefarious deed of troubling a pure Vaiṣṇava devotee. As Durvāsā was being harassed by the *sudarśana cakra* of Lord Viṣṇu, he came to his senses and understood that he was mistaken in considering a pure devotee to be less qualified than a mystic like himself. In the end, Durvāsā was excused by Mahārāja Ambarīṣa, who was naturally always forgiving to everyone. Durvāsā Muni, being relieved from his misconception of caste predominance, praised the Personality of Godhead and His sweet relationship with His pure devotee. He said, "Nothing is impossible for a pure devotee of the Personality of Godhead because simply by hearing His transcendental name, a person becomes purified of all vices." The purport is that if a person can become purified of all sins simply by hearing the Holy Name of Godhead, what is impossible for His servant who is constantly engaged in His service? Durvāsā Muni acknowledged the supremacy of a servant of Godhead over any kind of *yogi*, what to speak of a *jñānī* or *karmī* (empiric philosopher or fruitive worker).

The transcendental bliss that is enjoyed by a servant of the Personality of Godhead has been described by Śrī Yāmunācārya. He said, "O my Lord, when shall I feel myself to be Your absolutely faithful, bona fide servant, and live in transcendental cheerfulness by constantly obeying Your orders after being completely freed from all mental speculative desires?"

Sakhya-Premā

Lord Caitanya was satisfied by Rāmānanda's explanation of transcendental servitude to the Personality of Godhead, and He asked Rāmānanda to go still further. Rāmānanda then explained spontaneous loving service rendered by a friend of the Personality of Godhead. This is called *sakhya-premā* or the transcendental *rasa* of friendship with the Personality of Godhead.

rāya kahe—"sakhya-prema—sarva-sādhya-sāra"

Sakhya-premā is superior to *dāsya-premā* in the following respect: Although in *dāsya-premā* there is a transcendental relationship with Godhead as master and servant, it includes the sense that "God is my maker." Thus in *dāsya-premā* there is an awareness of the greatness of the Personality of Godhead, and as such *dāsya-premā* is mixed with a sense of fear and reverence for Him.

In *sakhya-premā,* the sense of fear and reverence is completely absent. On the contrary, a sense of equality prevails in the *sakhya-premā*. This sense of equality is an advance over the *dāsya-premā.* Here is a quotation from *Śrīmad-Bhāgavatam* (10.12.11) on the subject of *sakhya-premā*:

itthaṁ satāṁ brahma-sukhānubhūtyā
dāsyaṁ gatānāṁ para-daivatena
māyāśritānāṁ nara-dārakeṇa
sārdhaṁ vijahruḥ kṛta-puṇya-puñjāḥ

"The Personality of Godhead Śrī Kṛṣṇa, who is experienced by the empiric philosophers as an impersonal feeling of transcendental bliss, who is the Supreme Personality of Godhead to the devotees related with Him as master and servant, and who is an ordinary human child to the people under the illusion of the external energy, was playing in the *rasa* of friendship with the cowherd boys of Vraja who obtained that stage of life after many, many virtuous acts accumulated in many, many lives."

Vātsalya-Premā

Lord Caitanya approved of this advance and asked Rāmānanda to go still further in the development of transcendental relationships. *Sakhya-premā* is an advance in transcendental mellowness over *dāsya-premā,* but *vātsalya-premā,* parental affection, is still more advanced than *sakhya-premā.*

Rāmānanda Rāya thus described a stanza from *Śrīmad-Bhāgavatam* wherein the excellence of *vātsalya-premā* is described.

nandaḥ kim akarod brahman
śreya evaṁ mahodayam
yaśodā vā mahā-bhāgā
papau yasyāḥ stanaṁ hariḥ

"O *brāhmaṇa,* it is puzzling to try to understand what virtuous acts Nanda Mahārāja performed that he could have Hari (Śrī Kṛṣṇa) as his son. It is also puzzling to try to understand about Yaśodādevī, who was addressed by the Personality of Godhead Śrī Kṛṣṇa as 'Mother' and whose breast He sucked in filial affection." Here is another quote from the *Śrīmad-Bhāgavatam* (10.9.20):

nemaṁ viriñco na bhavo
na śrīr apy aṅga-saṁśrayā

prasādaṁ lebhire gopī
yat tat prāpa vimuktidāt

"Thus the blessing of the Personality of Godhead Śrī Kṛṣṇa, which was gained by the cowherd lady Yaśodādevī, was never expected by the demigods like Brahmā or Śiva or even by Lakṣmīdevī, who is the constant consort of the Personality of Godhead Nārāyaṇa."

This means that Śrīmatī Yaśodādevī and Nanda Mahārāja worshiped the Personality of Godhead with the conception of the 'sonhood of Godhead.' In Christianity the 'fatherhood of Godhead' is accepted, and in Hinduism there is worship of *Śakti,* the external energy of Godhead, the 'motherhood of Godhead.' Both of these shadows of *vātsalya-premā* are material or a product of the external energy. They are a sort of perverted representation of the real *vātsalya-premā,* because by such a material conception of 'fatherhood' or 'motherhood' of Godhead, the worshiper's aim is to extract service from the Almighty.

The spirit of enjoyment and the spirit of renunciation are the predominant factors of material existence. The enjoying spirit is cultivated by the *karmīs*, people engaged in fruitive activities, and the spirit of renunciation is cultivated by the *jñānīs*, empiric philosophers, who have become baffled by their engagement in fruitive activities. Both the *karmīs* and *jñānīs* are therefore materialists because both of them maintain the spirit of being served by the Absolute Truth. To satisfy their own conceptions, both of them demand something from the Absolute Truth.

The Absolute Truth is meant to be served by all living entities. He is not meant to serve the living entities. The living entities are mentioned in the *Bhāgavad-gītā* as the parts and parcels of the Absolute Truth. The parts and parcels are meant to render service to the whole. It is absurd for the parts and parcels to think of becoming one with the whole or to extract service from the whole. The part and parcel living entity, when unfit to render service, is detached from the whole. Therefore, the spirit of demanding service from the Absolute Whole is a symptom of being detached from the Absolute Whole, or, in other words, of being in the domain of the external energy of Godhead. Such a demanding policy of the materialists, through the conception of the 'fatherhood' or 'motherhood' of Godhead, is a slight attempt to revive their eternal relationships with Godhead; however, these conceptions are far from the conception of the 'sonhood of Godhead' as shown by Nanda and Yaśodā.

The conception of the 'sonhood of Godhead' is a cent percent spiritually pure transcendental *rasa*. There was no demand made by Nanda and Yaśodā on the Personality of Godhead. They offered pure and simple service to the Personality of Godhead by nursing Him as a baby. Under the influence of *yogamāyā*, the internal energy of Godhead, they thought of Śrī Kṛṣṇa as nothing more or less than their affectionate and dependent son. The service of parents for a dependent son is always spontaneous and unalloyed.

Mādhurya-Premā

Lord Caitanya admitted the superiority of *vātsalya-premā* over *sakhya-premā,* but He asked Rāmānanda to go still further in the realm of transcendental mellowness. Lord Caitanya said:

prabhu kahe—"eho uttama, āge kaha āra"
rāya kahe, "kāntā-prema sarva-sādhya-sāra"

"So far, you have certainly explained the gradual development of transcendental, eternal relationships with the Personality of Godhead very well. But above this conception of *vātsalya-premā* there is a supreme transcendental *rasa,* which is the topmost transcendental service." Upon hearing this suggestion of Lord Caitanya, Rāmānanda declared that a transcendental conjugal relationship with Godhead is the highest form of loving service rendered to the Personality of Godhead.

The process of developing a transcendental relationship with Godhead is understood gradually. By simply accepting the glories of the Personality of Godhead and establishing service to Him in the transcendental *rasa* of calmness, *śānta-premā,* the sentiment of love for Godhead as one's personal master is not developed. *Śānta-premā* is a stage of peaceful appreciation of the glories of the Personality of Godhead.

In *dāsya-premā* or transcendental servitude to Godhead, a sense of intimacy with Godhead is not developed. In both *sakhya-premā,* transcendental friendship with Godhead, and *vātsalya-premā,* parental affection, the sense of unrestricted approach for loving service is not developed. As such, the complete perfection of transcendental relationships is not found. The fullness of service, unchecked by all conventional restrictions, is only developed in *mādhurya-premā,* transcendental loving service in conjugal love.

Thus, on the order of Lord Caitanya, Rāmānanda began to explain the nature of *mādhurya-premā.* Rāmānanda quoted a verse from the *Śrīmad-Bhāgavatam* wherein Uddhava spoke of the fortune of Kṛṣṇa's cowherd girlfriends, who melted away in ecstasy when they heard Uddhava describe the activities of Śrī Kṛṣṇa. Uddhava said,

nāyaṁ śriyo 'ṅga u nitānta-rateḥ prasādaḥ
svar-yoṣitāṁ nalina-gandha-rucāṁ kuto 'nyāḥ
rāsotsave 'sya bhuja-daṇḍa-gṛhīta-kaṇṭha
labdhāśiṣāṁ ya udagād-vraja-sundarīṇām

"The transcendental happiness that was bestowed upon the beautiful damsels of Vraja, who got the opportunity to be embraced by the strong hands of Śrī Kṛṣṇa on the occasion of performing the *rāsa-līlā,* was never experienced even by Lakṣmī, who resides on the chest of the Personality of Godhead Nārāyaṇa. Neither was such pleasure ever felt by the angels of heaven whose bodies emanate the smell of lotus flowers. What to speak then of ordinary beauties?" (*Bhāg.* 10.47.60)

Quoting another passage from *Śrīmad-Bhāgavatam* (10.82.2), Rāmānanda said,

tāsām āvirabhūc chauriḥ
smayamāna-mukhāmbujaḥ
pītāmbara-dharaḥ sragvī
sākṣān manmatha-manmathaḥ

"Śrī Kṛṣṇa, who is the enchanter of Cupid, dressed in yellow, wore a garland of flowers, and all of a sudden appeared in His eternal smiling form in the midst of the cowherd girls, who were mourning in separation from Him after the pastime of the *rāsa-līlā*."

Thus Rāmānanda Rāya summarized all of the different transcendental relationships with Godhead. He said that all of these are means of gaining the favor of Śrī Kṛṣṇa. A devotee in a particular relationship with Godhead will consider that relationship the highest of all, but when all the transcendental relationships are scrutinized and compared from a neutral angle of vision, the difference of intensity can be estimated.

Upstarts

Presently, a class of *asuras* (ungodly people who are demoniac in nature) have ventured to become preachers of spiritual realization by propagating a novel theory that the Absolute Truth is a matter of personal realization and the particular type of realization one has does not matter. This idea has sprung up from demoniac thinking that directly denies any particular cause of the creation. A description of such *asuras* is given in the sixteenth chapter of the *Bhagavad-gītā*. The *asuras* do not believe in the existence of the Personality of Godhead, under whose direction the creation takes place.

According to the *asuras,* everything in the world is a matter of chance and there is no truth in the belief that God has created the universe. The different philosophical theories about the creation, put forward by atheists, are speculative gymnastic feats. Because they say that determining the Absolute Truth is a matter of personal realization, the so-called favor of Godhead can be achieved by any means that may be conceived of by a simple speculator. They say that there are as many ways of realizing God or the Absolute Truth as there are speculators in the world.

Rāmānanda Rāya is certainly not one of these speculators, and his mention of "various means of gaining the favor of Godhead" does not suggest that the transcendental favor of Godhead can be achieved by any speculative method of the empiric philosopher or the upstarts of spiritual fervor.

In the name of Lord Caitanya's cult of devotion, many speculators of the above nature have already sprung up. The "various means" as suggested by Rāmānanda is not an adjustment of the false means of achieving the favor of Godhead adopted by the imitation Caitanyaites. "Various means" are mentioned in connection with the perfect mellows of love, namely *śānta-premā, dāsya-premā, sakhya-premā, vātsalya-premā,* and *mādhurya-premā.*

The five transcendental *rasas* of loving service are possible only after one has transcended the stage of material impediments known as *anarthas* (unwanted things in the heart). Those who have no access to the transcendental service of Godhead wrongly think that manufactured processes are equal to the above-mentioned self-realized stages of love of Godhead. This misconception of the upstarts is but a sign of their misfortune.

Mellow of Sweetness

The analysis of the above-mentioned five transcendental *rasas* is also made in the *Bhakti-rāsamṛta-sindhu.* It is said there that the transcendental *rasas* are experienced in five progressive ways. Yet at a certain point, one *rasa* is experienced as the sweetest of all.

A practical analysis has been made by Śrīla Kṛṣṇadāsa Kavirāja Goswāmī in the following example: "Ether, air, fire, water, and earth are five different elements. Sound is experienced in ether. Sound and touch are experienced in air. Sound, touch, and form are experienced in fire. Sound, touch, form, and taste are experienced in water. And sound, touch, form, taste, and smell are experienced in earth. Earth has the qualities of all the elements. The analysis is that each elemental quality is developed through the other by gradual development, but the last one, namely earth, possesses all the qualities."

In the same way, the transcendental mellowness experienced in the stage of *śānta-premā* is developed in the stage of *dāsya-premā* and then *sakhya-premā*. It is further developed in *vātsalya-premā,* and lastly the complete development is manifested in the stage of *mādhurya-premā,* for *mādhurya-premā* includes all the *rasas* experienced in all the other devotional stages.

According to the *Śrīmad-Bhāgavatam* (10.82.45), the Personality of Godhead is completely obliged by the transcendental loving service rendered in the mood of *mādhurya-premā*:

mayi bhaktir hi bhūtānām
amṛtatvāya kalpate
diṣṭyā yad āsīn mat-sneho
bhavatīnāṁ mad-āpanaḥ

The Personality of Godhead said, "Loving devotional service unto Me is itself the eternal life of the living entity. My dear cowherd girls, the affection that you have in your hearts for Me is the only cause of achieving My favor."

In the *Bhagavad-gītā* (4.11) it is said,

ye yathā māṁ prapadyante
tāṁs tathaiva bhajāmy aham
mama vartmānuvartante
manuṣyāḥ pārtha sarvaśaḥ

The Personality of Godhead declares that He is experienced in proportion to the degree of one's surrender. The Lord reciprocates in His different manifestations with the particular feelings of His devotees.

Quacks of Spiritual Science

The materialistic philosophers of this world, by way of mental speculation, have decided that God is approachable by any means of spiritual cultivation. According to them, it does not matter whether the method is fruitive action, empiric philosophical speculation, mystic yoga, meditation, penance, or any other method; all of them will ultimately lead to the highest goal. The example that they generally put forward in support of their theory goes like this: "There may be several thoroughfares, and if any one of them is followed, surely one will reach the desired destination." More explicitly, they say that God is represented in various forms such as Lord Rāmacandra, the impersonal *Brahman*, Goddess Kālī, Durgā, Mahādeva, Gaṇeśa, and many others, and as such any one of them can be worshiped with equal value.

Another example they use in this connection is that a man may have many names and if he is called by any one of them, he replies to the call. These statements of the quacks of spiritual science are like the indistinct vocal attempt of a spiritual baby. The indistinct voice of a baby may be very sweet to the ear of mental speculators, but the bona fide spiritualists reject it as a foolish child's babbling.

Attachment for Demigods

The *Bhāgavad-gītā* (9.25) states:

yānti deva-vratā devān
pitṛn yānti pitṛ-vratāḥ
bhūtāni yānti bhūtejyā
yānti mad-yājino'pi mām

The worshipers of the demigods such as Gaṇeśa, Surya, and Indra will ultimately reach the abodes of such gods. They will go to the planets of those demigods respectively according to their worship, while only the devotee of Śrī Kṛṣṇa will reach the abode of Śrī Kṛṣṇa. Thus the mundaners avoid the *Bhāgavad-gītā*. They forget that they are under the influence of the conditions of the external energy. As such, they worship the demigods motivated by a desire for material gain and develop an illusory attachment for such demigods and thereby are thrown from the real path of progress—

reaching the Personality of Godhead. Being attached thus, the worshipers of different demigods are forced to circumambulate the different spheres of the material world and undergo the rigors of repeated birth and death.

Those who aspire to reach the Personality of Godhead and thereby worship Him by loving service will certainly reach Him. The real explanation is that one gets the result of the quality of their worship, and all the results are not the same, as conceived by the mundane speculators. Those who aspire after the results of their religiosity, economic development, sense gratification, and endeavors for salvation cannot expect to reach the same destination as the pure transcendental devotees. The result of religiosity is temporary happiness in the human life. The result of economic development is increased facility for sense gratification. And the result of sense gratification is frustration, which leads to the desire for liberation. The result of salvation is merging into the impersonal *Brahman*. But the result for the devotee of Śrī Kṛṣṇa is the attainment of the eternal service of the Personality of Godhead. The gulf of difference between these diverse results cannot be understood by the mundaners.

Mahāmāyā and Yogamāyā

Mahāmāyā, the mother or source of this material world, and the delegated demigods are but diverse external energies or agencies of the Supreme Personality of Godhead. Under the direction of the Personality of Godhead, these agencies perform their respective functions in the administration of the universal laws. That is the information we have from the *Bhagavad-gītā,* in which the Personality of Godhead declares that only under His direction does the material energy produce the material world, and the whole administration of the universes is thus controlled, ultimately by Him.

The internal energy of Godhead is different. That is also explained in the *Bhagavad-gītā*—there is another permanent energy of Godhead that is never destroyed, even after the annihilation of the whole cosmic manifestation. That internal energy is different from *mahāmāyā* and she is called *yogamāyā*.

The permanent universe is the creation of *yogamāyā*. Those who want unalloyed loving service to the Personality of Godhead must ask for the mercy of *yogamāyā*. Those who want to satisfy their own senses or those who desire to become one with the impersonal *Brahman* because of being baffled by the pursuit of sense gratification worship *mahāmāyā* or the predominating demigods respectively.

The damsels of Vraja worshiped *yogamāyā* to get the son of the King of Vraja as their husband or lover, while others within the system of material *varṇāśrama-dharma* worship *mahāmāyā*, the superintending Deity of the material world, to alleviate distress. There is a gulf of difference between the results of these two varieties of worship, and the attempt to equalize such diametrically opposed activities is like the jaundiced eye seeing everything as yellow. Such is the vision of the diseased person in ignorance.

The Name is Absolute

Sometimes a homely man is named "Cupid." In such a case, the name is without any significance. But this is never the case with the Personality of Godhead. Being the Absolute, all His different features are also absolute. There is no difference between Him, His names, and His features. He is known by different names. He is known as the impersonal *Brahman*, Paramātmā, the Almighty Creator, Nārāyaṇa, Gopīnātha, Kṛṣṇa, Govinda, and many other such names.

Although every name of the Absolute is absolute in itself, the worshiper of God as the Creator of the Universe cannot relish the same bliss as those who worship God as Nārāyaṇa. "The Creator of the Universe" is the name preferred by materialistic people, as it is suitable for their sense gratification. The conception of 'Creator' does not fully represent the conception of Godhead. The creation is a function of Godhead's external energy. If He is conceived of as the impersonal *Brahman*, we cannot get information about all of His potencies. His transcendental bliss, knowledge, qualities, and form are not fully represented in His impersonal feature. Paramātmā is also not fully representative of the conception of Godhead. In the *Bhāgavad-gītā* (18.61), Paramātmā is described as localized Godhead in the heart of all living beings; He is only a partial representation of the Personality of Godhead, Nārāyaṇa. Then again, the worshiper of Nārāyaṇa also cannot relish the transcendental bliss experienced in the service of Śrī Kṛṣṇa.

Rasābhāsa

The pure devotees of Śrī Kṛṣṇa do not wish to worship Nārāyaṇa, in whose personality the transcendental mellowness of Śrī Kṛṣṇa is somewhat covered. The cowherd girls never addressed Śrī Kṛṣṇa as "the husband of Rukmiṇī." That would be intolerable for them. Rukmiṇī-ramaṇa and Śrī Kṛṣṇa may be the same Personality of Godhead in the opinion of the mundaners, but They cannot be equally relished. If someone mixes up both of the above out of sheer ignorance, that is a defect in relishing transcendental mellowness called *rasābhāsa*. People who have some sense of the delicate transcendental nature of Godhead do not commit the mistake of *rasābhāsa* like those who form the society of ignorant people.

Not Possible to Reciprocate

Although the Personality of Godhead reciprocates accordingly with the dealings of His different devotees in different stages of loving service, He has declared His inability to reciprocate with the dealings of the *gopīs*, the damsels of Vraja who serve Him in the capacity of *mādhurya-premā*. Addressing the damsels of Vraja, the Personality of Godhead Śrī Kṛṣṇa said,

na pāraye 'haṁ niravadya-saṁyujāṁ
sva-sādhu-kṛtyaṁ vibudhāyuṣāpi vaḥ
yā mābhajan durjaya-geha-śṛṅkhalāḥ
saṁvṛścya tad vaḥ pratiyātu sādhunā

"My dear cowherd girls, your love for Me is spotlessly pure and it will not be possible for Me to reciprocate with the noble service you render to Me, not even in many future lives, because you have completely sacrificed the shackles of family life to come to Me. I am therefore unable to repay the debts I have incurred in accepting your love. You must therefore kindly be satisfied by your own deeds." (*Bhāg.* 10.32.21)

The beauty of Śrī Kṛṣṇa increases in the association of the cowherd girls of Vraja, although Śrī Kṛṣṇa Himself is the last word in all beauty. This is confirmed in the *Śrīmad-Bhāgavatam* (10.33.6):

tatrātiśuśubhe tābhir
bhagavān devakī-sutaḥ
madhye maṇīnāṁ haimānāṁ
mahā-mārakato yathā

"Although the Personality of Godhead who is the son of Devakī is the last word in beauty, when He is in the midst of the cowherd girls of Vraja, He appears like the most valuable jewel set within a network of golden filigree."

Lord Caitanya was now completely satisfied by the statement of Rāmānanda Rāya about *mādhurya-premā,* which is the culmination of transcendental loving service relationships with the Personality of Godhead. Still, He expected something more from Rāmānanda and asked him to go still further. At this most extraordinary request of Lord Caitanya, Rāmānanda was astonished. He knew no devotee who could know more than this. But as expert as he was, Rāmānanda began to go still further by the mercy of Lord Caitanya.

The Topmost Servitor

Having already discussed the superexcellent qualities of the transcendental mellowness known as *mādhurya-premā* and Śrī Kṛṣṇa's inability to repay the service of the spotlessly pure-hearted cowherd girls of Vraja, Rāmānanda then proceeded further in the same line in an attempt to discuss the service rendered by Śrīmatī Rādhārāṇī, the topmost servitor among all the cowherd girls.

Śrī Kṛṣṇa, the Absolute Supreme Personality of Godhead, is the full-fledged *ānanda-cinmoya-rasa-ujjvala-vigraha:* His eternal form fully displays transcendental existence, knowledge, and bliss by His own internal potency called the *hlādinī-śakti.* Śrīmatī Rādhārāṇī is the controlling Deity of that joyous energy of Godhead. The joyous nature of Śrī Kṛṣṇa's energy and Śrī Kṛṣṇa Himself are identical, but They appear separately for the purpose of enjoying each other. Therefore, Śrī Śrī Rādhā-Kṛṣṇa are two component parts of the same divine entity. Without Śrīmatī Rādhārāṇī, Kṛṣṇa is incomplete; and without Śrī Kṛṣṇa, Rādhārāṇī is incomplete. Thus these two cannot be separated from one another. They combine as one in Śrī Caitanya Mahāprabhu to fulfill this transcendental truth.

Most Magnanimous

It is very difficult to understand the *līlā* of Śrī Śrī Rādhā-Kṛṣṇa, but Lord Caitanya is the most liberal, magnanimous, merciful, and willing benedictor of all living beings in this age of Kali. He is readily distributing the highest secret of the spiritual world and only requires that we accept it.

Lord Caitanya has provided us with the easiest way to receive His topmost gift. The first qualification is that one should at once discard the idea of *sāyujya-mukti* or becoming one with the impersonal *Brahman.* The second qualification is that one should simply hear all these transcendental messages in a fully submissive mood from a person who is a bona fide devotee in the line of Śrīla Rūpa Goswāmī's disciplic succession. And the third and last qualification is that one be very pure in all one's dealings in life, remaining unaffected by the infectious influence of the age of Kali.

A person who has all of these three simple qualifications will have phenomenal success in entering into the plane of Lord Caitanya Mahāprabhu's unbounded mercy. Any deviation from the above-mentioned three qualities will completely close the door of entrance, regardless of how one may try to understand Him by the strength of one's mundane acquisitions. Without the above three qualifications nobody can enter into Lord Caitanya's *līlā*. Those who have tried to enter into it neglecting the necessary qualities are known as *āula, bāula, karttābhajā, neḍā, sakhī-bhekī, daraveśa, sāṇi, sahajiyā, smārta,* caste *goswāmīs, ativāḍi, cūḍādhārī, gaurāṅga-nāgarī,* and many others. Such persons may be considered worthless imitators of Lord Caitanya Mahāprabhu's *līlā.* Unfortunately, they are misleading the ignorant masses who are already condemned by the influence of Kali-yuga.

Not For Ordinary People

Śrīmatī Rādhārāṇī is the most important of all the *gopīs,* and Her specific loving service is the highest expression of *mādhurya-premā.* Therefore, it is better that the neophyte practitioners in the devotional field not try to understand the intimacies of Śrīmatī Rādhārāṇī's confidential service. However, expecting that submissive and bona fide devotees will understand Śrīmatī Rādhārāṇī's service in the future, these confidential discussions are described by Śrīla Kṛṣṇadāsa Kavirāja Goswāmī in his *Caitanya-caritāmṛta.*

Devotees who have been fortunate enough to rise to the spontaneous service of Godhead, *rāgānuga-bhakti,* and who have developed an attraction for *mādhurya-premā,* may follow in the footsteps of the confidential associates of Śrīmatī Rādhārāṇī and their assistants called the *mañjarīs.*

The ecstasy that was felt by Śrīmatī Rādhārāṇī when She met Uddhava in Vraja in Her mournful mood of separation from Śrī Kṛṣṇa is personified in Lord Caitanya. Nobody should imitate Lord Caitanya's transcendental feelings because it is impossible for a living being to reach that stage. However, at a stage of developed consciousness one can simply follow in His footsteps. These are the hints given by experienced and self-realized devotees in the line of Śrīla Rūpa Goswāmī.

Distinguished Cowherd Girl

Rāmānanda Rāya then explained a *śloka* from the *Padma Purāṇa*:

yathā rādhā priyā viṣṇos
tasyāḥ kuṇḍaṁ priyaṁ tathā
sarva-gopīṣu saivaikā
viṣṇor atyanta-vallabhā

"Śrīmatī Rādhārāṇī is the most beloved cowherd girl of Śrī Kṛṣṇa. Not only Śrīmatī Rādhārāṇī, but the lake known as Śrī Rādhā-kuṇḍa is as dear to Śrī Kṛṣṇa as Śrīmatī Rādhārāṇī Herself."

Rāmānanda Rāya then quoted another *śloka* from *Śrīmad-Bhāgavatam* (10.30.28):

anayārādhito nūnaṁ
bhagavān harir īśvaraḥ
yan no vihāya govindaḥ
prīto yām anayad rahaḥ

"My dear friends, the cowherd girl who has just been taken in privacy by Śrī Kṛṣṇa, leaving us all aside, must have rendered more valuable service to Him than ourselves."

Śrī Rādhā is the specific name of the distinguished cowherd girl who has rendered the most obliging services to Śrī Kṛṣṇa. On hearing these two statements by Rāmānanda, Lord Caitanya felt an ecstasy of His own and said to Rāmānanda:

prabhu kahe—āge kaha, śunite pāi sukhe
apūrvāmṛta-nadī vahe tomāra mukhe

"Please continue. I am feeling too much happiness by your mode of explanation. It is something like a transcendental river of bliss flowing from your tongue." Lord Caitanya added:

curi kari' rādhāke nila gopī-gaṇera ḍare
anyāpekṣā haile premera gāḍhatā nā sphure

"Śrī Kṛṣṇa stole away Śrīmatī Rādhārāṇī because the nature of love that He had for Her was disturbed in the presence of the other *gopīs*. If Kṛṣṇa can give up the company of all other *gopīs* for the sake of Śrīmatī Rādhārāṇī, I know that He is especially attached to Her love."

When the transcendental pastime of *rāsa-līlā* continued, Śrī Kṛṣṇa thought that in the presence of all the *gopīs,* confidential and secluded love affairs with Śrīmatī Rādhārāṇī would not be possible. He thought that in the presence of others the intensity of private love affairs could not be relished. For this reason, Śrī Kṛṣṇa abducted Śrīmatī Rādhārāṇī from within the assembly of all the other *gopīs* and became separated from them all.

The Search of Śrī Kṛṣṇa

Rāmānanda Rāya said that there is no comparison to Śrīmatī Rādhārāṇī's love within the universe. Śrīmatī Rādhārāṇī did not like to be equal with all the other *gopīs*. Thus in a mood of erotic anger, She left the arena of the *rāsa-līlā*. It was the desire of Śrī Kṛṣṇa that Śrīmatī Rādhārāṇī fulfill His necessity for *rāsa-līlā*, but when She went away, Śrī Kṛṣṇa became disturbed and in a mood of moroseness He left the *rāsa-līlā* arena to search for Śrīmatī Rādhārāṇī. Rāmānanda Rāya quoted two other *ślokas* from the *Gīta-govinda* (3.1, 2):

kaṁsārir api saṁsāra-
vāsanā-baddha-śṛṅkhalām
rādhām ādhāya hṛdaye
tatyāja vraja-sundarīḥ

itas-tatas tām anusṛtya rādhikām
anaṅga-vāṇa-vraṇa-khinna-mānasaḥ
kṛtānutāpaḥ sa kalinda-nandinī
taṭānta-kuñje viṣasāda mādhavaḥ

"The enemy of Kaṁsa (Śrī Kṛṣṇa) became afflicted with the desire to liberate His parents Vasudeva and Devakī from imprisonment in Mathurā and left the company of the beautiful damsels of Vraja, keeping Śrīmatī Rādhārāṇī within His heart.

"Being afflicted by the arrow of Cupid and unhappily regretting His mistreating Rādhārāṇī, Mādhava (Śrī Kṛṣṇa) began to search for Śrīmatī Rādhārāṇī along the banks of the Yamunā River. When He failed to find Her, he entered the bushes of Vṛndāvana and began to lament."

All the above statements are of a very, very high standard of transcendental pastimes of the Personality of Godhead and may appear to be like the ordinary stories of a hero and heroine. The whole activity may also appear like the lusty behavior of ordinary men and women, but this is the foolishness of the mundane conception. The complete picture is of transcendental loving service to the Personality of Godhead by the pure senses, completely freed from mundane designations and cleansed of all mundane affairs. Only the highest devotee, who is absolutely purified by the regulative principles of devotional service and who has attained the stage of realizing the degraded nature of mundane erotic activities, can relish these supramundane affairs, although they are described in language that is understandable to the general populace.

The cheerfulness of Lord Caitanya in relishing the above statements by Rāmānanda Rāya is the proof that they are the highest standard of transcendental expression. Therefore, readers should be careful not to bring these topics down to a level of mundane affairs.

Rāmānanda Rāya continued to explain that by a critical study of the above two *ślokas* we can know that the *rāsa-līlā* is performed in the company of innumerable cowherd girls, but, in spite of this, the Personality of Godhead prefers to remain specifically with Śrīmatī Rādhārāṇī. Knowing this, a devotee's heart becomes swollen with transcendental joy, which may be compared to a mine of nectar.

Hearing about all these transcendental love affairs, the hearts of experienced devotees are filled with an inexplicable supramundane joy. They feel that Śrī Kṛṣṇa is equally fond of all the *gopīs,* but He is specifically attracted by the clever and often contradictory dealings of Śrīmatī Rādhārāṇī. Thus She contributes the most to the *rāsa-līlā.*

By Śrīmatī Rādhārāṇī's Side

It is understood from the authoritative literatures, which describe the transcendental pastimes of Godhead, that in the arena of the *rasa-līlā* dance, Śrī Kṛṣṇa distributed Himself in His innumerable *prakāśa* expansions by keeping Himself between each of the cowherd girls. He also kept Himself by the side of Śrīmatī Rādhārāṇī. The *prakāśa* expansions of His transcendental body are all identical, but the personality by the side of Śrīmatī Rādhārāṇī is His original form, *svayam-rūpa*. Śrī Kṛṣṇa is equal to everyone in His general dealings, but due to the conflicting ecstatic love of Śrīmatī Rādhārāṇī there were opposing elements. This is described in the *Ujjvala-nīlamaṇi* as follows:

aher iva gatiḥ premṇaḥ
svabhāva-kuṭilā bhavet
ato hetor ahetoś ca
yūnor māna udañcati

"The curved ways of progressive love affairs appear like the movement of a snake. Further, two different kinds of anger, anger with a cause and anger without a cause, arise within the dealings of a young man and a young woman."

In pursuance of the above principles, Śrīmatī Rādhārāṇī in a mood of erotic anger left the arena of the *rāsa-līlā* with a feeling of devout attachment. Thus Śrī Hari also became mad after Her and perturbed in His mind out of anger without cause. Śrī Kṛṣṇa's desire was to enjoy the transcendental pastime of the *rāsa-līlā* in its fullness and the cornerstone of its whole construction was Śrīmatī Rādhārāṇī. Without Her presence, the *rāsa-līlā* is upset. Therefore, the absence of Śrīmatī Rādhārāṇī caused Śrī Kṛṣṇa to leave the arena and go in search of Her.

When Śrī Kṛṣṇa was unable to find Śrīmatī Rādhārāṇī after searching here and there, He became overwhelmingly afflicted by Cupid's arrow and began to deeply lament on account of Her absence. This fact proves that the transcendental heart of Śrī Kṛṣṇa is not satiated even by His enjoyment in the midst of so many millions of other cowherd girls. As such, the intensity of His love for Śrīmatī Rādhārāṇī is impossible to describe.

All the above statements regarding the transcendental *līlā* of Śrī Śrī Rādhā-Kṛṣṇa profusely delighted Lord Caitanya and He became completely satisfied by His meeting with Rāmānanda Rāya.

prabhu kahe—ye lāgi' āilāma tomā-sthāne
sei saba tattva-vastu haila mora jñāne

ebe se jāniluṅ sādhya-sādhana-nirṇaya
āge āra āche kichu, śunite mana haya
kṛṣṇera svarūpa' kaha 'rādhāra svarūpa'
'rasa' kon tattva, 'prema'—kon tattva-rūpa
kṛpā kari' ei tattva kaha ta' āmāre
tomā-vinā keha ihā nirūpite nāre

Lord Caitanya said to Rāmānanda, "I have now come to know the truth of the *līlā* of Śrī Kṛṣṇa and Śrīmatī Rādhārāṇī for which I approached you. I have understood the truth of the highest goal to be attained and also the means to attain it. Therefore, please explain the divine nature of Śrī Kṛṣṇa and also that of Śrīmatī Rādhārāṇī. Please also let me know the truth of the mellowness of supramundane love affairs. Nobody can explain all these except your good self. Therefore, I request you to do me this favor by your unbounded mercy."

Guru of Lord Caitanya

The method of approach and the manner of humility exhibited by Lord Caitanya to Rāmānanda is the ideal for approaching a bona fide *tattva-darśī* or a master of transcendental knowledge. This is confirmed in the *Bhāgavad-gītā* (4.34):

tad viddhi praṇipātena
paripraśnena sevayā
upadekṣyanti te jñānaṁ
jñāninas tattva-darśīnaḥ

In the *Bhāgavad-gītā,* it is recommended that one approach the spiritual master for supramundane knowledge under the protection of service and surrender accompanied by relevant inquiries. Lord Caitanya, as the ideal teacher and practical demonstrator of the teachings of the *Bhāgavad-gītā,* teaches us by His approach to Rāmānanda Rāya. He shows that a person desirous of knowing the transcendental science must not be proud of his material acquisitions of education and wealth, which are very insignificant to the transcendentally situated spiritual master from whom we should be very keen to understand the science of devotion.

If somebody approaches the bona fide spiritual master with the vanity of mundane pride in respect to his heredity, wealth, education, or personal beauty and without the necessary qualifications of surrender, service, and relevant inquiry, surely such a person will be honored outwardly by the spiritual master, but the spiritual master will decline to bestow transcendental knowledge upon the student who by his attitude of mundane vanity is rendered unqualified. Such a proud student is actually a *śūdra* and he has no access to spiritual knowledge for want of the necessary qualifications mentioned above. Thus the *śūdra* student, instead of availing himself to the mercy of the spiritual master, goes to hell as a result of his mundane vanity.

Rāmānanda Rāya was born in the family of a *śūdra* and was also a *gṛhasta* in terms of the system of *varṇāśrama-dharma.* Lord Caitanya appeared in the family of a highly cultured *brāhmaṇa* of Navadvīpa and was in the topmost rank of the *sannyāsa āśrama.* Therefore, in terms of the *varṇāśrama* system, Rāmānanda Rāya was in the lowest status while Lord Caitanya was in the highest status; yet, because Rāmānanda was a master in the art of transcendental knowledge, Lord Caitanya approached him as one should approach a guru. He did so for the benefit of us all.

True Student of Truth

Lord Caitanya descended into this mortal world as the ideal spiritual master, and thus His teaching is very significant. The students who really desire spiritual upliftment may carefully note all these dealings.

Rāmānanda Rāya, as a true Vaiṣṇava, always possessed natural humility, and thus when he was asked by Lord Caitanya he said,

rāya kahe—ihā āmi kichui nā jāni
tumi yei kahāo, sei kahi āmi vāṇī
tomāra śikṣāya paḍi yena śuka-pāṭha
sākṣāt īśvara tumi, ke bujhe tomāra nāṭa
hṛdaye preraṇa kara, jihvāya kahāo vāṇī
ki kahiye bhāla-manda, kichui nā jāni

"My Lord, I have no information of the transcendental world but I can simply speak that which You inspire me to utter. I am just like a parrot and I can repeat only that which You direct me to say. You are Yourself the Personality of Godhead and it is very difficult to understand what You do and how You play. The inspiration that You create in me and the vocabulary that You cause to come out of my mouth are known to You. I do not know myself what I speak and what I think."

Lord Caitanya, again in His mood of a true student of truth, replied to Rāmānanda Rāya,

prabhu kahe—māyāvādī āmi ta' sannyāsī
bhakti-tattva nāhi jāni, māyāvāde bhāsi
sārvabhauma-saṅge mora mana nirmala ha-ila

'kṛṣṇa-bhakti-tattva kaha,' tāṅhāre puchila
teṅho kahe—āmi nāhi jāni kṛṣṇa-kathā
sabe rāmānanda jāne, teṅho nāhi ethā
tomāra ṭhāñi āilāṅa tomāra mahimā śuniyā
tumi more stuti kara 'sannyāsī' jāniyā
kibā vipra, kibā nyāsī, śūdra kene naya
yei kṛṣṇa-tattva-vettā, sei 'guru' haya
'sannyāsī' baliyā more nā kariha vañcana
kṛṣṇa-rādhā-tattva kahi' pūrṇa kara mana

"I am a *māyāvādī sannyāsī* who is an atheist by nature. As such, I always float on My theory of *māyā* and *Brahman* without any entrance into devotional science. By the association of Sārvabhauma Bhaṭṭācārya, I was lucky enough to get My heart purified. When I asked him to speak about the transcendental topics of the *līlā* of Śrī Kṛṣṇa and Śrīmatī Rādhārāṇī, he asked Me to see you. He recommended you as the best among those who know this science and he regretted your absence at Purī. I have therefore come to you after hearing your glories from him. You are now praising Me because I am a *sannyāsī*, but it does not matter whether a person is a *brāhmaṇa*, a *sannyāsī*, or a *śūdra*. A person is thoroughly competent to become a bona fide spiritual master provided he knows the transcendental art and science of devotional activities. Therefore please do not try to avoid Me because I am a *sannyāsī*. Kindly fulfill My desire by fully describing the glories of the *līlā* performed by Śrī Kṛṣṇa and Śrīmatī Rādhārāṇī."

Beyond Varṇa and Āśrama

In the teachings of Lord Caitanya, especially in this perverted age of Kali, the passage mentioned above, wherein it says that it does not matter whether a person is a *brāhmaṇa, sannyāsī,* or a *śūdra,* is important. The qualification for a spiritual master is that he must be thoroughly conversant in the art and science of devotional service. This is revolutionary to the stereotyped, so-called spiritual mastership prevailing among the masses in India. The exploitative method is herein dealt a deadly blow and this truth is established by the devout followers of Śrī Caitanya Mahāprabhu's conception.

The fact is that a person who is thoroughly conversant about Śrī Kṛṣṇa can become a spiritual master either as an initiator or an instructor. It does not matter whether such a person is a *brāhmaṇa, kṣatriya, vaiśya,* or a *śūdra*. Nor does it matter whether he is a *brahmacārī, gṛhastha, vānaprastha,* or a *sannyāsī*. The only qualification of a spiritual master is his knowledge of the truth about Śrī Kṛṣṇa. The qualification certainly does not rest on his particular situation in terms of the system of *varṇāśrama-dharma*.

This order of Lord Caitanya, although apparently revolutionary to the non-progressive opportunists, is not at all against the injunctions of the scriptures. Following this principle, Lord Caitanya Himself took initiation from Śrīpād Īśvara Purī, and Lord Nityānanda Prabhu and Advaita Prabhu took initiation from Śrīpād Mādhavendra Purī Goswāmī. Rasikānānda Prabhu took initiation from Śrīla Shyāmananda Prabhu, who appeared in the family of a *non-brāhmaṇa,* and Śrī Ganga Nārāyaṇa Cakravartī and Śrī Rāmakṛṣṇa Bhaṭṭācārya took initiation from Śrīla Narottama dāsa Ṭhākura, who also happened to appear in the family of a *non-brāhmaṇa.* In the ancient literatures, it is written that there are no hereditary considerations for becoming a spiritual master.

In the *Mahābhārata* and other historical literatures, there are innumerable examples of non-hereditary gurus and determination of caste by quality and action rather than by birth. In the *Śrīmad-Bhāgavatam* (7.11.35), it is said that a person should be classified as belonging to a particular *varṇa* or caste in terms of his qualification:

yasya yal-lakṣaṇaṁ proktaṁ
puṁso varṇābhivyañjakam
yad anyatrāpi dṛśyeta
tat tenaiva vinirdiśet

According to *Bhāgavad-gītā,* a really qualified *brāhmaṇa* possesses nine qualities, a *kṣatriya* seven qualities, a *vaiśya* three qualities, and a *śūdra* only one quality. So, wherever the particular qualities are found or developed, the person possessing these particular qualities should be regarded as such. Accepting this formula from the scriptures, the Vaiṣṇava accepts a spiritual master upon his becoming conversant in the knowledge of Śrī Kṛṣṇa. The qualities of a *brāhmaṇa* appear naturally, and, as such, a thoroughly conversant spiritual master cannot be anything but a qualified *brāhmaṇa*. The false notion that without being a caste *brāhmaṇa* a person cannot become a spiritual master is therefore a misconception. A person born in the family of a *śūdra* can become a spiritual master if he has acquired the necessary knowledge about Śrī Kṛṣṇa.

Sometimes it is seen that a pure Vaiṣṇava does not undergo the formalities of the system of *varṇāśrama-dharma* by accepting the regulative principles thereof, but that does not mean that he is not a *brāhmaṇa* or a bona fide spiritual master. The Vaiṣṇavas determine the *varṇa* and *āśrama* of a person simply by their symptoms and not by their birth. Foolish people are unable to recognize such qualified Vaiṣṇavas, and as such Lord Caitanya distinctly emphasizes all the above mentioned points. There is no difference in essence between the regulative principles found in the *Hari-bhakti-vilāsa* and the statements of Lord Caitanya. The difference is concocted by the mental speculations of ignorant men.

Who is an Ācārya

Some foolish students have accepted the statements of Lord Caitanya conditionally. According to them, the spiritual master fully conversant with the science of Kṛṣṇa, yet not born in a *brāhmaṇa* family, can be an instructing spiritual master, but not an initiating spiritual master. They do not know that there is hardly any difference between the two classes of spiritual masters. According to them, a caste initiator or caste *goswāmī*, by dint of his hereditary blood lineage, becomes the real spiritual master, while a person knowing all about Śrī Kṛṣṇa can only become an instructor. They foolishly think that the position of the initiating spiritual master is greater than that of the instructing spiritual master. However, the matter is very clearly and conclusively discussed in the *Caitanya-caritāmṛta* (*Ādi-līlā* 1.47):

śikṣā-guruke ta' jāni kṛṣṇera svarūpa
antaryāmī, bhakta-śreṣṭha—ei dui rūpa

"One should know the instructing spiritual master to be the Personality of Kṛṣṇa. Śrī Kṛṣṇa manifests Himself as the Supersoul and as the greatest devotee of the Lord."

In the *Manu-saṁhitā,* the qualification of an *ācārya* is described as follows: "A spiritual master is a twice-born *brāhmaṇa* able to train his disciple to instruct others on the *Vedas*." In the

Vāyu Purāṇa, the *ācārya* is described as follows: "One who knows the essence of the scriptures, establishes the truth of them, and conducts his activities according to the regulative principles of the scriptures is thus known as an *ācārya.*"

The *ācārya* or spiritual master is an empowered incarnation of the Personality of Godhead. He is not to be considered a plenary portion of Godhead, but at the same time the spiritual master is certainly very near and dear to Godhead. The *ācārya* appears before the disciple as the bona fide representative of Godhead. Such an *ācārya* has no duty other than to serve the Personality of Godhead and give shelter to the willing disciple on Godhead's behalf.

If a person becomes a so-called spiritual master without being engaged wholly in the service of the Personality of Godhead, nobody should accept him as guru and his activity should not be recognized. A guru's character must be fully representative of the Personality of Godhead, and this will be demonstrated by his full-time engagement in the service of Godhead. A real *ācārya* is sometimes envied by the sense-gratifying masses. However, the *ācārya* is a nondifferent extension of the transcendental body of the Personality of Godhead. Anyone envying such a spiritual master will certainly suffer the consequence of being bereft of the Personality of Godhead's blessings.

The spiritual master, although the eternal servitor of Lord Caitanya, is always to be respected as much as Lord Caitanya. The spiritual master is the personality who exhibits the nature of Lord Caitanya. It should never be concluded that the spiritual master is exactly one and the same with Godhead as the *māyāvādī* philosophers think. The Vaiṣṇavas accept the spiritual master in terms of *acintya-bhedābheda-tattva,* simultaneously one with and different from the Personality of Godhead.

Śikṣā and Dīkṣā

A spiritual master who gives instruction about the regulative principles of devotional service is called the *śikṣā-guru* or the instructing spiritual master. A person who is not engaged in the service of the Personality of Godhead and is addicted to ill habits cannot be a spiritual master. The instructing spiritual master is of two kinds. They are: (1) a self-realized soul constantly engaged in the service of the Personality of Godhead, and (2) a soul in pure consciousness who is constantly offering helpful directions favorable to the service of Godhead. Instruction in the service of the Lord is also of two kinds: (1) instruction on the object of service, and (2) instruction on the regulative principles of service.

The spiritual master who connects the living entity with the Personality of Godhead Śrī Kṛṣṇa by initiation is called the *dīkṣā-guru* or the initiating spiritual master. There is no difference between the initiating spiritual master and the instructing spiritual master. Both are the object of shelter for the disciple and both are *āśraya vigraha* or the personality under whose shelter the eternal relationship with Godhead is established and the process of approaching Godhead by service is learned. To think of one spiritual master as purer than the other is offensive. The symbolic initiating spiritual master is Śrīla Sanātana Goswāmī, who initiates the devotees into their service to Madana-mohana. Śrīla Rūpa Goswāmī is the instructing spiritual master, who instructs the devotee with his verses in the *Bhakti-rāsamṛta-sindhu* regarding the service of Śrī Śrī Rādhā-Govinda. Nobody should therefore think of Sanātana Goswāmī as being greater than Rūpa Goswāmī or vice versa. Both of them are our spiritual masters and engage us in the transcendental loving service of Godhead.

When Lord Caitanya mentioned the word *guru,* spiritual master, He meant both the *śikṣā-guru* and the *dīkṣā-guru* and not just one of them.

Not a Vaiṣṇava—Not a Guru

According to *Hari-bhakti-vilāsa,* a pure devotee of Godhead is never a *śūdra.* On the other hand, one who is not engaged in the service of the Personality of Godhead is definitely a *śūdra,* even though such a person may be born in the family of any *varṇa* other than *śūdra.* A *brāhmaṇa* of the standard of *varṇāśrama-dharma,* although expert in all the details of the six specific functions of the scriptures, cannot be accepted as a spiritual master if he is not a Vaiṣṇava. But if an untouchable *caṇḍāla* (dog-eater) becomes a Vaiṣṇava, he can be accepted as a spiritual master. A pure devotee of Godhead, although born in the family of a *śūdra,* can be the spiritual master of all the other three *varṇas.*

Rāmānanda Rāya, being always conscious of his transcendental task, is never subjected to the deluding energy of Godhead. He could understand the feelings of Lord Caitanya, and by His will, Rāmānanda wanted to proceed further. He said,

rāya kahe—āmi—naṭa, tumi—sūtra-dhāra
yei mata nācāo, taiche cāhi nācibāra
mora jihvā—vīṇā-yantra, tumi—vīṇā-dhārī
tomāra mane yei uṭhe, tāhāi uccāri

"My Lord, I am a dancing doll and You are the wire-puller. Let me dance as you wish. My tongue is like the *vīṇā* (a stringed musical instrument) and You are playing upon it. Kindly let me vibrate the sound that You desire to produce."

Rāmānanda continued:

parama īśvara kṛṣṇa—svayaṁ bhagavān
sarva-avatārī, sarva-kāraṇa-pradhāna
ananta vaikuṇṭha, āra ananta avatāra
ananta brahmāṇḍa ihāṅ—sabāra ādhāra
sac-cid-ānanda-tanu, vrajendra-nandana
sarvaiśvarya-sarvaśakti-sarvarasa-pūrṇa

īśvaraḥ paramaḥ kṛṣṇaḥ, sac-cid-ānanda-vigrahaḥ
anādir ādir govindaḥ, sarva-kāraṇa-kāraṇam
vṛndāvane 'aprākṛta navīna madana'
kāma-gāyatrī kāma-bīje yāṅra upāsana

"Śrī Kṛṣṇa is the Supreme Personality of Godhead, the cause of all causes. He expands Himself in His innumerable plenary portions known as incarnations. He is the fountainhead of innumerable Vaikuṇṭha planets, innumerable incarnations, and innumerable universes. He is the eternal form of transcendental existence, knowledge, and bliss. He is known as the son of the King of Vraja. He is complete in Himself with all opulences, all powers, and all divine *rasas*. He is, as stated in the *Brahma-saṁhitā,* the Supreme Primeval Lord and the cause of all causes. Śrī Kṛṣṇa is the transcendental Cupid and the resident of Śrī Vṛndāvana. He is worshiped by the transcendental sounds produced by the pure utterances of *kāma-gāyatrī* and *kāma-bīja.*"

Vṛndāvana Eternal

Vṛndāvana, the residence of Śrī Kṛṣṇa, is described in the *Brahma-saṁhitā* (5.56):

śriyaḥ kāntāḥ kāntaḥ parama-puruṣaḥ kalpa-taravo
drumā bhūmiś cintāmaṇi-gaṇa-mayī toyam amṛtam
kathā gānaṁ nāṭyaṁ gamanam api vaṁśī priya-sakhī
cid-ānandaṁ jyotiḥ param api tad āsvādyam api ca
sa yatra kṣīrābdhiḥ sravati surabhībhyaś ca sumahān
nimeṣārdhākhyo vā vrajati na hi yatrāpi samayaḥ
bhaje śveta-dvīpaṁ tam aham iha golokam iti yaṁ
vidantas te santaḥ kṣiti-virala-cārāḥ katipaye

Everything is cognizant in the transcendental abode of Vṛndāvana. Although appearing in the material world, it exists eternally, even after the annihilation of the material world. The *Bhagavad-gītā* (8.20) confirms this statement. In Vṛndāvana, the cowherd girls are all enjoyed by Śrī Kṛṣṇa, and He is the only enjoyer there because He is the Supreme Person. The trees in Vṛndāvana are all desire trees and the land is made of *cintāmaṇi*, desire-fulfilling touchstones. The water of Vṛndāvana is nectar, the words of conversation are themselves sweet songs, walking in Vṛndāvana is a dance, and the flute is eternally the constant companion of Śrī Kṛṣṇa. The luminaries in the sky are transcendental and blissful. With this in mind, we should always try to understand Vṛndāvana. In Vṛndāvana, even a moment is never lost because no moment passes away, and, as such, there is not a limited conception of the future either.

The Vṛndāvana-dhāma that we can experience in this mortal world is therefore a subject of deep study, and the significance of Vṛndāvana is known only to the purest devotees. Let us therefore worship Śrī Vṛndāvana.

The Vṛndāvana-dhāma that manifests in the material world is not realized by our material senses, which are always prone to enjoy matter. When we are inspired by the proper attitude of transcendental service to Madana-mohana, we can know the actual

Vṛndāvana. Because it is very difficult to understand, Śrīla Narottama dāsa Ṭhākura taught us by his actions to cry for the mercy of Lord Nityānanda Prabhu. By the mercy of Lord Nityānanda, we can be free from the consciousness of trying to enjoy this material world. This enjoying spirit is known as *saṁsāra-vāsanā*. When one is freed from the *saṁsāra-vāsanā,* one is freed from focusing entirely on eating, sleeping, fearing, and other sense-gratifying habits. When this is done, the mind of the devotee is purified from all infections of matter, and in such a state of mind one can see the true Vṛndāvana-dhāma situated in this mortal world.

Cupid and the Kāma-Gāyatrī

The eternal Cupid, Śrī Kṛṣṇa, is eternally distinct from the material Cupid. The material Cupid produces pleasure only temporarily, but then lulls one into material dullness in just the next moment. But the eternal Cupid is ever-awakening and the transcendental pleasure is ever-increasing in ever-renewing developments. Such pleasure is eternally-existing and is not subject to the laws of material nature. The transient pleasure derived from the material Cupid is an enjoyable object to the materialists, but the transcendental Cupid is served eternally because He is Śrī Kṛṣṇa, the Personality of Godhead Himself.

Gāyatrī means that which delivers one from the clutches of material hankerings. By chanting the *kāma-gāyatrī, klīṁ kāma-devāya vidmahe puṣpa-bāṇāya dhīmahī tan no 'naṅgaḥ pracodayāt,* the transcendental sound composed of twenty-four and a half letters, one is connected with the service of Madana-mohana (*kāma-devāya*). The nature of practical service is realized in connection with Govinda (*puṣpa-bāṇāya*). And in the perfect stage of service, one is connected with Gopīnātha (*anaṅgaḥ*), the attractor of the cowherd girls.

The description of the *kāma-gāyatrī* in the *Brahma-saṁhitā* is vivid. The *kāma-gāyatrī* was first chanted by Lord Brahmā before he created the material universes. His pure consciousness was awakened in the matter of his relationship, action, and ultimate goal in the service of the Personality of Godhead. When he became absorbed in the chanting of the transcendental sound of the *kāma-gāyatrī,* he acquired the ability to create the universe, and as such he composed the *Brahma-saṁhitā* in praise of the glories of Lord Govinda, the Personality of Godhead.

The scientific arrangement of the *kāma-gāyatrī* is described in the *Brahma-saṁhitā*. It says that the supramundane *kāma-gāyatrī* combined with the *kāma-bīja* (the nucleus of transcendental love) is the transcendental means of worship by which the eternally youthful transcendental Cupid, Madana-mohana, is served. Śrī Viśvanātha Cakravartī Ṭhākura has explained the symbolic representation of the *kāma-bīja 'kliṁ,'* with reference to the *Bṛhad Gautamīya-tantra*, as follows: K is Kṛṣṇa, the supreme aggressive male, who possesses a form embodying full eternity, knowledge, and bliss; the letter I is Rādhā, the supreme receptive female, who is eternally the Vṛndāvaneśvarī, or the most majestic Princess of Śrī Vṛndāvana; the letter L is celebrated as *ānandātmaka-prema-sukha,* or the happiness of Rādhā and Kṛṣṇa's mutual ecstatic love in the form of pure blissful joy; and the Ṁ is the expression of *cumban-ānanda-mādhurya,* or the ecstatic sweetness of Their most blissful kiss. When the *kāma-bīja* is added to the *gāyatrī,* it becomes the transcendental prayer for worshiping Śrī Śrī Rādhā-Kṛṣṇa.

Rāmānanda Rāya continued to speak: "Śrī Kṛṣṇa has multi-energies, three of which are prominent. They are known as the internal energy, external energy, and marginal energy; or the potency of full knowledge of life, the potency of darkness or ignorance, and the potency of the living being." In the *Viṣṇu Purāṇa,* these potencies are also mentioned. The internal energy and the marginal energy are referred to as the superior energies while the external energy or the potency of darkness is called the inferior energy.

Hlādinī, Sandhinī, and Samvit

Śrī Kṛṣṇa is originally a person full with transcendental existence, knowledge, and bliss. His internal energy or the potency of full knowledge is manifested in three diverse ways: *hlādinī, sandhinī,* and *samvit,* which represent transcendental bliss, existence, and knowledge respectively. In the *Viṣṇu Purāṇa,* the same is confirmed as follows: "O Lord, in You who are all-pervading, the *hlādinī, sandhinī,* and *samvit* energies are all cognizant. Your parts and parcels, the living entities, have obtained the powers that are the perverted forms of *hlādinī, sandhinī,* and *samvit.* They have done so under the influence of the three qualities of the external energy, because the living entities are prone to be influenced by the deluding energy known as *māyā*. However, in You these three energies are transcendental to the qualities of *māyā*."

Who is Topmost

The *hlādinī* energy means the pleasure potency and by this energy, which is His own, Śrī Kṛṣṇa becomes enthused and relishes His happy moods. The *hlādinī* energy is the cause of transcendental happiness for the devotees engaged in the transcendental service of Godhead. The *hlādinī* energy in Her very concentrated form is the embodiment of love of Godhead, which produces the emotions of transcendental bliss and knowledge. This transcendental love of Godhead in its mature state is named *mahābhāva* and Śrīmatī Rādhārāṇī is *mahābhāva* personified. She is thus described in the *Ujjvala-nīlamaṇi* (4.3) as follows:

tayor apy ubhayor madhye
rādhikā sarvathādhikā
mahābhāva-svarūpeyaṁ
guṇair ativarīyasī

"Among the cowherd girls, Śrīmatī Rādhārāṇī and Śrīmatī Candrāvalī are the principal *gopīs*. Out of these two, Śrīmatī Rādhārāṇī is the topmost because Her position is that of *mahābhāva* or the highest stage of transcendental love of Godhead. No other cowherd girl possesses such high qualities as Śrīmatī Rādhārāṇī."

premera 'svarūpa-deha'—prema-vibhāvita
kṛṣṇera preyasī-śreṣṭhā jagate vidita

"Śrīmatī Rādhārāṇī is love of Godhead personified. She is made of pure love of Godhead. She is therefore celebrated in the universe as the most beloved of Śrī Kṛṣṇa."

The *Brahma-saṁhitā* (5.37) describes this as follows:

ānanda-cinmaya-rasa-pratibhāvitābhis
tābhir ya eva nija-rūpatayā kalābhiḥ
goloka eva nivasty akhilātma-bhūto
govindam ādi-puruṣaṁ tam ahaṁ bhajāmi

"I worship the primeval Lord Govinda, who in His original form resides in His abode named Goloka along with the transcendental cowherd girls, who are always inspired by the feelings of transcendental bliss and knowledge. That Govinda is the all-pervading Godhead."

Śrīmatī Rādhārāṇī is further described by Śrīla Raghunātha dāsa Goswāmī in his *Premāmbhoja-maranda*:

> The identity of Śrīmatī Rādhārāṇī is the personified service of Śrī Kṛṣṇa to fulfill His every desire. Her associates such as Lalitā, Viśākhā, and other friends are the symbols of Her expression of such intimate service. The manifestation of Her first youthfully blooming appearance is the result of Her using the cosmetic made out of the affection of Śrī Kṛṣṇa. Her first (morning) bath is in the nectarean water of youthful energy. The gradual development of Her youthful beauty is the nectar of Her bath in the afternoon. Her evening bath is completed in the water of full-grown youth, and thus the three stages of Her youthful growth is compared with Her bath thrice daily classified under the names of *kāruṇyāmṛta, tāruṇyāmṛta,* and *lāvaṇyāmṛta*. This is the description of Her transcendental body.

Qualities of Śrīmatī Rādhārāṇī

As far as Her dress is concerned, it is described in two parts. One is made of Her youthful blush of modesty woven with *śyāma* or black colored threads turned into a bluish covering, and the second is called *uttaria* which is red due to extreme attachment for the company of Śrī Kṛṣṇa.

Her breasts are covered by Her *sari* in the form of affection and anger toward Kṛṣṇa. Her personal beauty is compared to *kuṅkuma* (a special kind of cosmetic) and Her friendship with Her associates is compared to sandalwood pulp. The sweetness of Her calm sobriety is compared to camphor. These three ingredients decorating the body of Śrīmatī Rādhārāṇī—*kuṅkuma,* sandalwood pulp, and camphor—are ever-increasingly glowing as Her youthful beauty.

Outwardly, She is very clever and contradictory while at heart She is submissive. She speaks with cruel words to Her lover, yet Her heart is revealed by the flow of tears from Her eyes. This emotion is called *dhīrādhīrātmaka*. The degrees of this particular emotion vary in intensity and are called *praghoṣa*, *madhya*, and *mugdha* respectively.

Her lipstick is the reddish color of Her lips due to Her deep attraction for Śrī Kṛṣṇa. The outward symptoms of Her transcendental sentiments such as cheerfulness, laughing, shivering, and crying are Her constant companions. Her different qualities may be divided into four categories, namely: (1) qualities pertaining to Her person, (2) qualities pertaining to Her words, (3) qualities pertaining to Her mind, and (4) qualities pertaining to Her relationship with others. She possesses six qualities in regard to Her person, three in regard to Her words, two in regard to Her mind, and six in regard to Her relationship with others. The description of these different qualities is very vividly given in the *Ujjvala-nīlamaṇi.* To avoid expansion of this literature, we will not elaborate on this subject at this time.

Śrīmatī Rādhārāṇī always bears in Her heart the sentiment of *prema-vaicittya*, a feeling of the fear of separation even when She is in the company of Her consort. This is due to Her being very softhearted. She is eternally a young girl between 16 and 20 years of age. This period is called *kaiśora*. She is always accustomed to moving along with Her hands resting on the shoulders of Her friends, the cowherd girls. She is always being lovingly attended by Her female friends and Her mind is always full of Her transcendental pastimes with Śrī Kṛṣṇa. Her constant cheerfulness is the fragrance of Her body and She is constantly sitting on the bedstead of Her peculiar pride due to constantly remembering Śrī Kṛṣṇa.

Constant remembrance of the name, fame, and qualities of Śrī Kṛṣṇa are the earrings decorating Her body. The glories of Śrī Kṛṣṇa's name, fame, and qualities are always inundating Her speech. She keeps Śrī Kṛṣṇa enlivened by the celestial drink of the incessant chanting of His qualities. In short, She is the reservoir of pure love of Kṛṣṇa and She is full and complete with all the necessary qualifications in this regard. She is the perfect symbolic representation of pure love of Godhead. This fact is described in the *Govinda-līlāmṛta* (11.122) in the form of questions and answers:

kā kṛṣṇasya praṇaya-janibhūḥ śrīmatī rādhikaikā
kāsya preyasy anupama-guṇā rādhikaikā na cānyā
jaihmyaṁ keśe dṛśi taralatā niṣṭhuratvaṁ kuce 'syā
vāñchā-pūrtyai prabhavati hare rādhikaikā na cānyā

Q: Who is the generating source of the love of Śrī Kṛṣṇa?
A: It is Śrīmatī Rādhikā only.
Q: Who is qualitatively the dearest to Śrī Kṛṣṇa?
A: Again, it is Śrīmatī Rādhārāṇī and nobody else. Śrīmatī Rādhārāṇī's hair is very curly, Her eyes are always moving to and fro, Her breasts are firm, and as such it is She alone who can fulfill all the desires of the all-attractive Hari.

yāṅra saubhāgya-guṇa vāñche satyabhāmā
yāṅra ṭhāñi kalā-vilāsa śikhe vraja-rāmā
yāṅra saundaryādi-guṇa vāñche lakṣmī-pārvatī
yāṅra pativratā-dharma vāñche arundhatī
yāṅra sadguṇa-gaṇane kṛṣṇa nā pāya pāra
tāṅra guṇa gaṇibe kemane jīva chāra

Rāmānanda Rāya concluded the descriptive qualities of Śrīmatī Rādhārāṇī by saying that She is envied by Satyabhāmā for Her unique fortune, and from Her alone the damsels of Vraja have learned the art of attracting a lover. Even Pārvatī and Lakṣmī, who are superexcellently beautiful, desire to possess Her qualities and beauty and rise to the level of Her chastity. Even Śrī Kṛṣṇa fails to calculate the qualities of Śrīmatī Rādhārāṇī. Therefore, how is it possible for any mortal being to estimate Her qualities?

On hearing these statements by Rāmānanda Rāya, Lord Caitanya said:

prabhu kahe—jāniluṅ kṛṣṇa-rādhā-prema-tattva
śunite cāhiye duṅhāra vilāsa-mahattva

"I have come to know the essence of love between Śrīmatī Rādhārāṇī and Śrī Kṛṣṇa. Now I wish to hear something about Their transcendental pastimes."

Qualities of Śrī Kṛṣṇa

Rāmānanda Rāya replied that Śrī Kṛṣṇa is *dhīra-lalita,* a person who is very clever, always youthful, expert in joking, free from all anxieties, and very submissive to His beloved. His characteristics are manifested always in His transcendental erotic pastimes. Thus He is constantly engaged in enjoyment with Śrīmatī Rādhārāṇī, making a perfection of the frolicsome age of *kaiśora.* This stage of Śrī Kṛṣṇa's engagement is described by Śrīla Rūpa Goswāmī as follows:

vācā sūcita-śarvarī-rati-kalā-prāgalbhyayā rādhikāṁ
vrīḍā-kuñcita-locanāṁ viracayann agre sakhīnām asau

tad-vakṣoruha-citra-keli-makarī-pāṇḍitya-pāraṁ gataḥ
kaiśoraṁ saphalī-karoti kalayan kuñje vihāraṁ hariḥ

"Śrī Kṛṣṇa perfectly enjoys the age of His adolescence by His pastimes with Śrīmatī Rādhārāṇī in the bowers of Vṛndāvana. He takes advantage of the cowherd girls by His expertise in the art of painting. He made Śrīmatī Rādhārāṇī close Her eyes in shame before Her friends by speaking words of Their lovemaking on the previous night. Then, while She was almost unconscious in a swoon, Śrī Kṛṣṇa, showing the highest limit of cleverness, painted Her breasts with various types of *makaras* (mystical fish)."

Topmost Love Affairs

On hearing these words, Lord Caitanya said:

prabhu kahe—eho haya, āge kaha āra
rāya kahe—ihā va-i buddhi-gati nāhi āra

"Yes, this is all right, but please go still further." Rāmānanda replied, "I think my intelligence is unable to go any further!" The stage that is yet to be described is *prema-vilāsa-vivarta,* the feeling of original attraction matured by the feeling of separation. "I do not know if such a description will be to Your satisfaction or not." Saying this Rāmānanda sang his own composition, the purport of which is as follows:

pahilehi rāga nayana-bhaṅge bhela
anudina bāḍhala, avadhi nā gela
nā so ramaṇa, nā hāma ramaṇī
duṅhu-mana manobhava peṣala jāni'

e sakhi, se-saba prema-kāhinī
kānu-ṭhāme kahabi vichurala jāni'
nā khoṅjaluṅ dūtī, nā khoṅjaluṅ ān
duṅhukeri milane madhya ta pāṅca-bāṇa
ab sohi virāga, tuṅhu bheli dūtī
su-purukha-premaki aichana rīti

"O, when We first met each other, the attraction was awakened by simple sight, and such attraction knows no bounds in the course of its growth, because that attraction was due to Our personal inclination. Neither Kṛṣṇa nor Myself is the cause of such spontaneous attraction but it awakened and pierced Our minds in the form of Cupid. We are now separated from one another. O My dear friend, if you think that Śrī Kṛṣṇa has completely forgotten Me, tell Him that at the first sight We never required any negotiation, neither did We search for any messages. Cupid himself was the agent of Our meeting. But alas, at this time, O My friend, you are doing the job of a messenger when Our attraction is more desirable than before." This sort of feeling during separation of the lover and the beloved is called *prema-vilāsa-vivarta,* which is the topmost sentiment in loving affairs.

Here is another heartfelt description of the same *prema-vilāsa-vivarta* by Śrīla Rūpa Goswāmī in his *Ujjvala-nīlamaṇi*:

rādhāyā bhavataś ca citta-jatunī
svedair vilāpya kramād
yuñjann adri-nikuñja-kuñjara-pate
nirdhūta-bheda-bhramam
citrāya svayam anvarañjayad iha
brahmāṇḍa-harmyodare
bhūyobhir nava-rāga-hiṅgula-bharaiḥ
śṛṅgāra-kāruḥ kṛtī

"O, the king of the pirates (Śrī Kṛṣṇa) resided in the bowers of Govardhana Hill! The Creator of the Universe, who is very much expert in the art of decoration, has melted the casing of your heart and that of Śrīmatī Rādhārāṇī with the perspiration of transcendental symptoms and emotions, and thereby removed the misconception of duality. By such wonderful activities, He has painted both of your hearts in order to play wonders upon the universe."

The explanation of the sentiment of *prema-vilāsa-vivarta* can only be realized in a pure state of consciousness freed from all material conceptions. This transcendental subject matter is not to be realized in a state of consciousness that is either grossly or subtly influenced by the material body and mind. External consciousness in relation to material intelligence and mind is different from the pure soul. The mellowness of this transcendental subject is relished by the senses engaged in the divine service of the Personality of Godhead.

Positive Consciousness

The pure state of consciousness enjoyed in the transcendental service of Godhead is only partially manifested in the impersonalists through their negation of material engagement. The impersonal negative conception is simply an antidote for material misconception, it has no positive standing. Such a state of consciousness may be somewhat enlightening, but it cannot reach the positive consciousness of the soul in its pure state. Love of Godhead is a pure and positive transcendental subject. The attraction for matter is transient and inferior, and therefore it is best described as only passing for love. The apparent happiness of the material world is really unhappiness. However, the transcendental unhappiness experienced in the *prema-vilāsa-vivarta* has nothing to do with the unhappiness of the material conception.

In concluding this explanation of *prema-vilāsa-vivarta,* the highest stage of transcendental relationships, Lord Caitanya said,

prabhu kahe—'sādhya-vastura avadhi' ei haya tomāra
prasāde ihā jāniluṅ niścaya
'sādhya-vastu' 'sādhana' vinu keha nāhi pāya
kṛpā kari' kaha, rāya, pābāra upāya

"Now I understand the topmost limit of the ultimate goal of life. This has been possible by your grace. The goal cannot be reached without the endeavor of the devotee and the mercy of a pure devotee. Please therefore let me now know the means of reaching this topmost goal." Rāmānanda continued,

rāya kahe—yei kahāo, sei kahi vāṇī
ki kahiye bhāla-manda, kichui nā jāni
tribhuvana-madhye aiche haya kon dhīra
ye tomāra māyā-nāṭe ha-ibeka sthira
mora mukhe vaktā tumi, tumi hao śrotā
atyanta rahasya, śuna, sādhanera kathā
rādhā-kṛṣṇera līlā ei ati gūḍhatara
dāsya-vātsalyādi-bhāve nā haya gocara
sabe eka sakhī-gaṇera ihāṅ adhikāra
sakhī haite haya ei līlāra vistāra
sakhī vinā ei līlā puṣṭa nāhi haya
sakhī līlā vistāriyā, sakhī āsvādaya
sakhī vinā ei līlāya anyera nāhi gati
sakhī-bhāve ye tāṅre kare anugati
rādhā-kṛṣṇa-kuñjasevā-sādhya sei pāya
sei sādhya pāite āre nāhika upāya

"My Lord, I do not know the means of approaching the ultimate goal of life, but I speak to You whatever You desire me to speak. I do not know if I am speaking correctly or incorrectly. Nobody in the three worlds will not dance according to Your wish. In fact, You speak through my mouth, and it is wonderful that You are the audience as well. Therefore, let me say that the transcendental pastimes of Śrīmatī Rādhārāṇī and Śrī Kṛṣṇa are extremely mysterious and confidential. Even those who are ardently engaged in the service of *dāsya, sakhya,* or *vātsalya rasas* cannot enter into the essence of Their pastimes. Only the eternal associates of Śrīmatī Rādhārāṇī, the cowherd girls of Vraja, have the authority to enter into this mystery because this transcendental pastime develops in their association. "The fulfillment of the sweetest of all transcendental pastimes depends on the activities of Śrī Rādhā's female associates. It is they alone who expand these pastimes and relish their development. Therefore, if anyone wants to reach this stage of transcendental life, he has to do so in the ardent service of such female associates. Only one who follows this principle can become a servitor of Śrīmatī Rādhārāṇī and Śrī Kṛṣṇa in the groves of Śrī Vṛndāvana. There is no other alternative in this regard."

Deeper Happiness

In the *Govinda-līlāmṛta* (10.17), the following description is given:

vibhur api sukha-rūpaḥ sva-prakāśo 'pi bhāvaḥ
kṣaṇam api na hi rādhā-kṛṣṇayor yā ṛte svāḥ
pravahati rasa-puṣṭiṁ cid-vibhūtīr iveśaḥ
śrayati na padam āsāṁ kaḥ sakhīnāṁ rasa-jñaḥ

"The transcendental pastimes of Rādhā and Kṛṣṇa are as self-effulgent as the Personality of Godhead Himself. Yet as the Almighty Godhead is glorified by His manifestation of diverse energies and potencies, the pastimes of Rādhā and Kṛṣṇa are glorified in the association of the *sakhīs* or female friends of Śrīmatī Rādhārāṇī."

The activities of the *sakhīs* are very wonderful. They do not desire any personal enjoyment with Śrī Kṛṣṇa but become happy only by uniting the Divine Couple. By uniting Śrīmatī Rādhārāṇī with Śrī Kṛṣṇa, the *sakhīs* enjoy a thousand times more happiness than they would derive by direct contact with Śrī Kṛṣṇa. This is another mystery of the transcendental pastimes of Rādhā and Kṛṣṇa.

Śrīmatī Rādhārāṇī is the desire creeper embracing the desire tree of Śrī Kṛṣṇa, and the *sakhīs* are the leaves, twigs, and flowers of that desire creeper. So naturally when the desire creeper is watered at the root by the nectarean water of the pastimes of Śrī Kṛṣṇa, the leaves and twigs and flowers of the desire creeper are automatically nourished. The *sakhīs* therefore do not require any separate arrangement for their enjoyment. On the other hand, the happiness of the flowers and leaves is greater than the original creeper. This is explained in the *Govinda-līlāmṛta* (10.16):

sakhyaḥ śrī-rādhikāyā vraja-
kumuda-vidhor hlādinī-nāma-śakteḥ
sārāṁśa-prema-vallyāḥ kisalaya-
dala-puṣpādi-tulyāḥ sva-tulyāḥ
siktāyāṁ kṛṣṇa-līlāmṛta-rasa-
nicayair ullasantyām amuṣyāṁ
jātollāsāḥ sva-sekācchata-guṇam
adhikaṁ santi yat tan na citram

"There is no utility in watering the leaves and flowers of a tree without watering the root of the tree. The leaves and flowers are automatically nourished by watering the root of the tree. Similarly, without the unity of Śrīmatī Rādhārāṇī and Śrī Kṛṣṇa, there is no happiness for the *sakhīs*. When Rādhā and Kṛṣṇa are united, the happiness of the *sakhīs* is thousands and thousands of times greater than when they are personally associating with Kṛṣṇa."

Great Mystery

There is another mystery within these transcendental pastimes, and it is that Śrīmatī Rādhārāṇī arranges for the uniting of Her associates with Śrī Kṛṣṇa, although the *sakhīs* have no such desire. By doing this, Śrīmatī Rādhārāṇī enjoys more happiness than by Her personally uniting with Śrī Kṛṣṇa and for this reason the *sakhīs* accept this arrangement for Her happiness. By all these mutual arrangements of Śrī Rādhā and the *sakhīs*, Śrī Kṛṣṇa becomes still more happy, and therefore the whole arrangement causes Rādhā and Kṛṣṇa to become even more enlivened in their transcendental pastimes.

The natural divine love of the cowherd girls for Śrī Kṛṣṇa is never to be considered as or compared to material lust. The two, love and lust, are explained in similar terms because there appears to be a similarity between them, but the *Bhakti-rāsamṛta-sindhu* (1.2.285) explains otherwise:

premaiva gopa-rāmāṇāṁ
kāma ity agamat prathām
ity uddhavādayo 'py etaṁ
vāñchanti bhagavat-priyāḥ

"People customarily describe and understand the love of the cowherd girls for Śrī Kṛṣṇa in the light of mundane lust, but in fact it is different because such a standard of love for Śrī Kṛṣṇa was desired even by the highest devotees like Uddhava and others."

Mundane lust is meant for one's personal enjoyment; transcendental love of Godhead is meant for the happiness of the Supreme Personality Śrī Kṛṣṇa. There is therefore a very wide gulf of difference between the two.

The cowherd girls of Vraja had no desire for self-satisfaction by personally contacting Śrī Kṛṣṇa, yet they were always ready to render all varieties of services for the benefit of Śrī Kṛṣṇa. Anything short of this spirit amounts to lust. As confirmed in the *Śrīmad-Bhāgavatam,* mundane desire is mundane lust. In the *Vedas,* the three modes of nature—goodness, passion, and ignorance—are described in different terms according to one's desire for different benefits—followers, sons, wealth, and so on. All these are but different categories of mundane lust. Such lust is presented in the flowery language of the *Vedas* as religiosity. Lust is called by different names: altruism, *karma-kāṇḍa,* fruitive work, social obligations, the desire for liberation, family tradition, affection for kinsmen, and fear of chastisement and rebuke from relatives. All these are different forms of lust passing in the name of religiosity. There is nothing in these activities except one's own sense gratification.

Surrender

In the *Bhagavad-gītā,* the final instruction is to give up all varieties of religion and follow the Personality of Godhead without reservation. In the beginning of the *Bhagavad-gītā,* the Personality of Godhead proclaimed that He descends to the earth whenever there is a rise of irreligious activities. He does so to protect the faithful, eradicate the unbelievers, and reestablish the principles of religiosity.

The two declarations mentioned above seem contradictory. The Personality of Godhead descends on earth to protect religiosity, but advises Arjuna to give up all varieties of religion. The explanation, however, is very clear. Complete surrender unto the will of the Personality of Godhead without any reservation is the factual principle of religiosity. All other activities, such as altruism, are not in fact religious. As such, the Personality of Godhead advises Arjuna to give them up. They are all different forms of mundane lust, gorgeously presented in the dress of religiosity.

Therefore, a transcendental conviction of feeling oneself to be the eternal servitor of Godhead and following this conviction means to follow the orders of Śrī Kṛṣṇa as He has advised in the *Bhagavad-gītā*. Whenever there is the feeling that one is the enjoyer of one's own activities, such actions are to be understood as different forms of mundane lust.

To surrender fully unto the desire of Śrī Kṛṣṇa does not turn one into a lifeless machine without any impetus. Rather, the feeling of being eternally engaged in the service of Śrī Kṛṣṇa gives one transcendental impetus for carrying out the will of Godhead through the divine medium of the spiritual master, who is identical in purpose with Śrī Kṛṣṇa. This is only possible when one is inspired by pure love of Godhead called *vyavasāyātmikā-buddhi*, supramundane intelligence that assures success in spiritual activities.

Imitators

The artificial way of decorating oneself in the dress of a *sakhī*, as is done by a class of mundaners called *sakhībhekī* or *gaurāṅga-nāgarī*, is not inspired by supramundane intelligence. Such artificial decoration of the body, which is meant for annihilation, certainly cannot please the transcendental senses of Śrī Kṛṣṇa. It is therefore a mundane wishful desire of the less intelligent, easygoing pseudodevotees, and as such it cannot reach the transcendental stage of the cowherd girls of Vraja.

We have already discussed in detail that the forms of Śrīmatī Rādhārāṇī and Her various female associates called the *sakhīs* are composed of divine substance and their activities are therefore meant for the service of Śrī Kṛṣṇa. Their activities are never to be compared with the superficial activities in the material world. Śrī Kṛṣṇa is the all-attractive Personality of Godhead known as the enchanter of the universe, and Śrīmatī Rādhārāṇī is known as the enchanter of the enchanter of the universe. The imitative endeavors of a mundaner to become a *sakhī* is strictly forbidden by Śrīla Jīva Goswāmī in his commentary on the *Bhakti-rāsamṛta-sindhu*. The real devotee may thus be warned not to imitate the dress of a *sakhī* as a means of *bhajana* or worship. Such activity is offensive and strictly forbidden.

The transcendental feelings of the cowherd girls mentioned in the *Śrīmad-Bhāgavatam* (10.31.19) are as follows:

yat te sujāta-caraṇāmburuhaṁ staneṣu
bhītāḥ śanaiḥ priya dadhīmahi karkaśeṣu
tenāṭavīm aṭasi tad vyathate na kiṁ svit
kūrpādibhir bhramati dhīr bhavad-āyuṣāṁ naḥ

"O my dear, Your lotus feet, which are very soft and are placed on our hard breasts, are now treading over the forest of Vṛndāvana and thereby receiving pain on account of stepping on the fine particles of stone. This fact is giving us anxiety because You are our very life." This example is the standard sentiment of the cowherd girls of Vraja and demonstrates that their very life is meant for the service of Śrī Kṛṣṇa without any tinge of an idea for sense gratification.

There are 64 different items of regulative devotional service. The devotee gradually develops the right to enter into the transcendental service of Godhead by implicit faith in the observance of the regulative principles. The intense eagerness to serve like the eternal associates of Śrī Kṛṣṇa, such as the cowherd girls, gives the devotee the right to serve Śrī Kṛṣṇa in that way. For this ardent service of Godhead, one is required to give up the practice of the mundane regulative principles of *varṇāśrama-dharma.*

Rāgānugā

In the transcendental abode of Vraja, the eternal residence of Śrī Kṛṣṇa, the inhabitants serve Śrī Kṛṣṇa in different mellows of loving service. Raktaka Parśada serves in the mellow of *dāsya-premā*. Madhumaṇgala Sakhā, Śrīdāmā, and Sudāmā serve in the mood of *sakhya-premā,* while Nanda and Yaśodā serve Śrī Kṛṣṇa in the mellow of *vātsalya-premā.* Any devotee who is attracted by any of the transcendental moods of service will obtain their desired goal at the time of perfection. A vivid example of this is the *śrutis* (the personified *Upaniṣads*). The *śrutis* were convinced that the transcendental loving service of Śrī Kṛṣṇa is not obtainable without following in the footsteps of the cowherd girls in Vraja. At that time, they adopted the spontaneous service of *rāgānugā* in pursuance of the footsteps of the *gopīs* with the aim of achieving *premā* for the son of the King of Vraja.

The *śrutis,* who obtained the transcendental service of Godhead by following in the footsteps of the *gopīs,* are described in the *Śrīmad-Bhāgavatam* (10.87.23):

nibhṛta-marun-mano 'kṣa-dṛḍha-yoga-yujo hṛdi yan
munaya upāsate tad arayo 'pi yayuḥ smaraṇāṭ
striya uragendra-bhoga-bhuja-daṇḍa-viṣakta-dhiyo
vayam api te samāḥ samadṛśo 'ṅghri-saroja-sudhāḥ

"The enemies of the Personality of Godhead, who remembered Him constantly with an inimical feeling, entered into the impersonal *Brahman* effulgence, which is also obtained by the empiric philosophers and mystics by the process of controlling the mind and the senses strictly by yoga practice and meditating upon the impersonal *Brahman*. But the cowherd girls, the damsels of Vraja, were hypnotized by the poisonous beauty of the snakelike arms of Śrī Kṛṣṇa, and thus they obtained the nectar of His lotus feet. We have also followed the path of the cowherd girls and are thus drinking the nectarean juice of the lotus feet of the Personality of Godhead."

The purport of this verse is that the *śrutis* followed the path of the *gopīs* and when they reached perfection they obtained bodies like those of the cowherd girls. After obtaining such transcendental bodies, they were able to enjoy the company of Śrī Kṛṣṇa in spiritual bliss.

Changing the Body

Advancement of material science in the field of medical surgery has made it possible to change the body of a human being from male to female or from female to male by surgical operation. The desire to change the body in this way is a kind of mundane lust. This lusty idea is a perverted reflection of the transcendental idea of changing the body as in the case of the *śrutis*. The idea of changing the body from one form to another is quite possible even by way of the materialistic mind. Therefore, by spiritual development the possibility of changing the body for the better is even greater.

The conclusion of the above-mentioned spiritual perfection is described in the *Śrīmad-Bhāgavatam* (10.9.21):

nāyaṁ sukhāpo bhagavān
dehināṁ gopikā-sutaḥ
jñānināṁ cātma-bhūtānāṁ
yathā bhaktimatām iha

"Śrī Kṛṣṇa, who is the son of Śrīmatī Yaśodādevī, is more easily available to persons engaged in spontaneous devotional service than to persons engaged in empiric philosophical speculations."

One who therefore accepts the example set by the cowherd girls of Vraja and always meditates upon the transcendental pastimes of Śrī Śrī Rādhā-Kṛṣṇa day and night while living in Vraja and serving Them there will ultimately obtain the body of a *sakhī* and directly serve Rādhā and Kṛṣṇa.

An Eternal Life of Ecstasy

The supramundane body is transcendental to the gross and subtle bodies of the living entity and it is suitable for rendering loving service to Śrī Śrī Rādhā-Kṛṣṇa. Transmigration of the soul from one body to another takes place in material existence according to the living entity's fruitive activities, which are carried out in relation to the three modes of nature. In the *Bhagavad-gītā,* the transmigration of the soul is vividly described. The mind carries the soul to another body just as the air carries aromas. At the time of death, one's state of mind is very important in this connection. The mind is prone to be absorbed in the particular kind of thinking, feeling, and willing that it has always done in relation to its daily activities.

The state of the mind at the time of leaving the body depends on the modes of thinking, feeling, and willing. Devotees are advised to think continuously, day and night, about the transcendental pastimes of Rādhā and Kṛṣṇa, so that their minds will be absorbed with that type of thinking, feeling, and willing. As such, it will be possible for the living entity to enter the kingdom of Rādhā and Kṛṣṇa to directly associate with Them for rendering loving service in the particular sentiment that he cultivated continually during his life.

In material existence, the mind is always conditioned to think about material enjoyment. Therefore, the mind has to be engaged in contemplating the transcendental subject matter that has no connection with the three modes of nature. The divine pastimes of Rādhā and Kṛṣṇa and the activities of the cowherd girls of Vraja are above the three qualities of material nature. When the mind is engaged in thinking, feeling, and willing in connection with such transcendental subjects, the living entity is sure to ultimately get the service of Rādhā and Kṛṣṇa.

The *deva-vratā*, people who are situated in the mode of goodness, worship the demigods such as Brahmā and Śiva and attain the abodes of such demigods. The *pitṛ-vratās*, people who are situated in the mode of passion for enjoying the material world and who worship the *pitṛs,* forefathers who have passed away, attain the different abodes of the *pitṛs*. The *bhūtejyās*, animal and ghost worshipers, who are situated in the mode of darkness and ignorance, also attain their respective destinations in the material world. But the devotees of the Personality of Godhead Śrī Kṛṣṇa attain His supreme abode, which is eternal. No one ever returns after attaining that abode.

All other spheres of attainment are considered temporary abodes because they are either vanquished after a limited duration of time or the residents of those abodes have to come back again to this earth after they have exhausted the results of their previous pious activities. As far as the *bhūtejyās* are concerned, they are doomed to hover on this earth or in even lower regions of the universe.

Lord Caitanya offers all people in the age of Kali, who are by nature very unfortunate in every respect, the highest benefit of life. As such, those who take this opportunity will be considered the most fortunate souls. By following the principles of devotional activities as propounded by Rāmānanda Rāya under the order of Lord Caitanya, every human being can attain the eternal life of ecstasy in the company of the Personality of Godhead in different transcendental *rasas* as are enjoyed by the denizens of Vraja or Goloka Vṛndāvana, the eternal abode of Śrī Kṛṣṇa.

No Entrance for Lakṣmīdevī

Without pursuing the footsteps of the *gopīs*, no one can obtain the spiritual body of a *sakhī* and render service to Śrī Kṛṣṇa, even if the devotional service is rendered in the mood of opulence. A vivid example of this is Śrī Lakṣmīdevī, who desired entrance into the transcendental pastimes of the *rāsa-līlā* of Śrī Kṛṣṇa. However, because Lakṣmīdevī did not follow in the footsteps of the cowherd girls of Vraja, she did not get entrance.

This statement of Rāmānanda Rāya caused Lord Caitanya to melt in complete ecstasy and thus He embraced him in His arms. Both Rāmānanda Rāya and Lord Caitanya were overflowing with tears of transcendental joy. The whole night was thus passed in divine conversation, and when the morning came, both Rāmānanda and Lord Caitanya went about their respective engagements.

As Lord Caitanya was leaving, Rāmānanda fell at his feet and fervently requested Him in the following way:

'more kṛpā karite tomāra ihāṅ āgamana
dina daśa rahi' śodha mora duṣṭa mana
tomā vinā anya nāhi jīva uddhārite
tomā vinā anya nāhi kṛṣṇa-prema dite'

"You have come here to bestow Your Divine Grace upon me; therefore, please remain here for at least ten days and see to it that my polluted mind is corrected. There is no one in the world but You who can deliver the fallen souls and there is no one in the world except You who can bestow upon them the transcendental mellowness of love of Godhead."

Lord Caitanya replied,

prabhu kahe—āilāṅa śuni' tomāra guṇa
kṛṣṇa-kathā śuni, śuddha karāite mana
yaiche śuniluṅ, taiche dekhiluṅ tomāra mahimā
rādhā-kṛṣṇa-premarasa-jñānera tumi sīmā
daśa dinera kā-kathā yāvat āmi jība'
tāvat tomāra saṅga chāḍite nāriba
nīlācale tumi-āmi thākiba eka-saṅge
sukhe goṅāiba kāla kṛṣṇa-kathā-raṅge

"I came to you after hearing of your reputation of pure devotion in order to purify My mind by hearing the transcendental message of Śrī Kṛṣṇa. I have just verified My information about you upon seeing and hearing you. You are the zenith of transcendental knowledge regarding the pastimes of Rādhā and Kṛṣṇa. As such, it will not be possible for Me to ever leave your company, what to speak of after ten days or so. We shall both live at Nīlācala (Jagannātha Purī) together and pass our time in perfect happiness always talking about the subject of the divine pastimes of Rādhā and Kṛṣṇa."

Perfect Questions and Answers

Thus Rāmānanda Rāya and Lord Caitanya separated from one another in the morning and in the evening they met again. The meeting took place in a secluded area and the talks began in the same manner of question and answer, with Lord Caitanya questioning and Rāmānanda answering.

Q: What is the essence of learning in the field of educational activities?

A: There is no superior quality of learning than the knowledge pursued in regard to devotional service to Śrī Kṛṣṇa.

Q: What is the highest fame?

A: The highest fame of a living being is a reputation of being a devotee of Śrī Kṛṣṇa.

Q: What is the most valuable possession of life among all the assets of the world?

A: One who has transcendental love for Rādhā and Kṛṣṇa is to be considered the richest person in the world.

Q: What is the most grievous type of sorrow among all the sorrows and distresses of life?

A: There is no greater type of sorrow than the unhappiness created by separation from devotees of Śrī Kṛṣṇa.

Q: Who is most perfectly liberated among all the liberated souls of the universe?

A: One who has transcendental love for Śrī Kṛṣṇa is the greatest of all liberated souls.

Q: What is the best song that a person can sing?

A: The essence of all songs is the singing of the transcendental glories of Rādhā and Kṛṣṇa.

Q: What is the highest benefit of life that a person can seek?

A: There is no greater gain in life than the association of devotees engaged in the service of Śrī Kṛṣṇa.

Q: Who is to be remembered constantly by the living being?

A: One should always think of the transcendental name, fame, and qualities of Śrī Kṛṣṇa.

Q: What should the living being meditate on?

A: The most perfect type of meditation is to meditate upon the lotus feet of Rādhā and Kṛṣṇa.

Q: Where should the living being reside exclusively, leaving all other residential quarters?

A: One should live in Vṛndāvana, where the transcendental pastimes of *rāsa-līlā* are perpetually performed.

Q: What should the living entity hear about, leaving aside all other topics?

A: The reciprocal loving pastimes of Rādhā and Kṛṣṇa are the only subject matter for aural reception by the living entity.

Q: What is the most worshipable object among all those to be worshiped?

A: The topmost worshipable object is the combined names of Rādhā and Kṛṣṇa.

Q: Where do persons go who aspire after liberation or sense enjoyment respectively?

A: The first person attains a body that is immovable (such as a stone or mountain), and the other attains a celestial body. (According to Gautama Buddha, liberation means to become like a stone, without any sense perception. That is the culmination of Buddhist philosophy.)

The above questions and answers contain the essence of all transcendental knowledge confirmed in the authoritative scriptures.

Most Learned Fellow

The gradual development of educational activities should be estimated in the following manner: *brahma-vidya* or knowledge of the spirit soul is superior to the knowledge of the physical world; knowledge about the Personality of Godhead is superior to the knowledge of the impersonal *Brahman* or spirit; and knowledge of Śrī Kṛṣṇa and His pastimes is superior to the knowledge of the Personality of Godhead Viṣṇu.

In the *Śrīmad-Bhāgavatam,* it is said that the highest work is that which will satisfy the senses of Hari, and the highest education is to teach about Him. One who has learned the nine different processes of devotional service—hearing, chanting, remembering, serving the Lord's lotus feet, worshiping, praying, becoming a servant, embracing the Lord in friendship, and fully surrendering unto Him—is to be considered the most learned fellow.

Fame

The fame a person receives because of being a devotee of Śrī Kṛṣṇa is described in the authoritative scripture *Garuḍa Purāṇa*:

kalau bhāgavataṁ nāma
durlabhaṁ naiva labhyate

brahma-rudra-padotkṛṣṭaṁ
guruṇā kathitaṁ mama

"I have heard from my spiritual master that in the age of Kali it will be very difficult to find a person who is famous because of being a devotee of Śrī Kṛṣṇa, although such a position is better than the position of Brahmā or Śiva."

Śrī Nārada Muni has said,

janmāntara-sahasreṣu
yasya syād buddhir īdṛśī
dāso 'haṁ vāsudevasya
sarvāl lokān samuddharet

"A person who considers himself the eternal servant of the Personality of Godhead Vāsudeva (a conception that is achieved after thousands and thousands of births) can deliver all the fallen souls in material existence."

In the *Bhagavad-gītā,* it is also confirmed that a person who is actually a *mahātmā* or great soul, having thoroughly understood that Vāsudeva is the Lord of all the universes, is very rarely found. After many, many births of acquiring knowledge, he surrenders unto Śrī Kṛṣṇa, the Personality of Godhead.

In the *Ādi Purāṇa,* it is said that the liberated souls, including the *śrutis,* follow the pure devotees of Śrī Kṛṣṇa. In the *Bṛhan-nāradīya Purāṇa* it is stated:

adyāpi ca muni-śreṣṭhā brahmādyā api devatāḥ

"Until now even the best among the *munis* (sages) or the demigods like Brahmā and others do not understand the influence of the devotee who has completely surrendered to the transcendental service of Viṣṇu."

In the *Garuḍa Purāṇa* it is stated:

brāhmaṇānāṁ sahasrebhyaḥ satra-yājī viśiṣyate
satra-yāji-sahasrebhyaḥ sarva vedānta-pāragaḥ
sarva-vedānta-vit-koṭyā viṣṇu-bhakto viśiṣyate
vaiṣṇavānāṁ sahasrebhya ekānty eko viśiṣyate

"Out of many, many thousands of *brāhmaṇas*, one who is expert in the performance of sacrifices is considered the best. Out of many thousands of such experts in the performance of sacrifices, one who has surpassed all the knowledge in the *Vedas* is considered the best. Out of all those persons who have excelled in the studies of the *Vedas*, a person who is a devotee of Viṣṇu, the Personality of Godhead, is considered the best. And out of many, many thousands of such worshipers of Viṣṇu, one who is a pure Vaiṣṇava or an exclusive devotee of Śrī Kṛṣṇa is the best because only he will attain the highest abode called *Paraṁdhāma*, which is described in the *Bhagavad-gītā* by Śrī Kṛṣṇa Himself."

In the *Śrīmad-Bhāgavatam,* it is also said that the purpose of acquiring knowledge of all the *śrutis* and of endeavoring in all the other ways of spiritual culture is that one will become addicted to the process of hearing the transcendental qualities, name, and fame of Mukunda (Śrī Kṛṣṇa).

In the prayers of the *Nārāyaṇa-līlā,* it is said that a pure devotee does not desire to be situated even in the position of a Brahmā if he is devoid of the devotional service of Godhead. Rather, the pure devotee prefers to become even a small insect if such a life is engaged in the devotional service of Godhead.

All Are Not Equal

The fame of Prahlāda Mahārāja as a devotee of Godhead is described in the *Skanda Purāṇa* by Lord Śiva: "Not even I can know Śrī Kṛṣṇa as He is. Only the devotees know Him, and of all the devotees, Prahlāda is the best."

In the *Bṛhad-bhāgavatāmṛta,* Sanātana Goswāmī says that above Prahlāda, the Pāṇḍavas are still better devotees, and the Yadus are better than the Pāṇḍavas. Out of all the Yadus, Uddhava is the best devotee, and the damsels of Vraja are even better than Uddhava. Therefore, they are the topmost of all devotees.

In the *Bṛhad-vāmana,* Brahmā spoke to the *ṛṣis* as follows:

ṣaṣṭi-varṣa-sahasrāṇi
mayā taptaṁ tapaḥ purā
nanda-gopa-vraja-strīṇāṁ
pāda-reṇūpalabdhaye

"I tried my best by undergoing austerity for 60 thousand years in order to be able to get the feet-dust of the damsels of Vraja, the cowherd boys, and King Nanda. Yet I did not get the blessings of the dust of their feet. Therefore, I think that myself, Śiva, and Lakṣmī are not at all equal to them."

In the *Ādi Purāṇa,* the Personality of Godhead said,

na tathā me priyatamo
brahmā rudraś ca pārthiva
na ca lakṣmīr na cātmā ca
yathā gopī-jano mama

"There is nobody dearer to Me than the cowherd damsels of Vraja—not even Brahmā, Śiva, Lakṣmī, or even My own Self."

Follow Śrīla Rūpa Goswāmī

Among all the inhabitants of Vraja, Śrīmatī Rādhārāṇī is the dearest of all. Śrīla Rūpa Goswāmī is the most confidential servitor of Śrīmatī Rādhārāṇī, and is therefore very dear to Lord Caitanya. The followers of the footsteps of Śrīla Rūpa Goswāmī are known as the Rūpānuga devotees of Śrī Kṛṣṇa. Such Rūpānuga devotees are eulogized in the *Śrī Caitanya-candrāmṛta (127)* as follows:

āstāṁ vairāgya-koṭir bhavatu
śama-dama-kṣānti-maitry-ādi-koṭis
tattvānudhyāna-koṭir bhavatu
vā vaiṣṇavī bhakti-koṭiḥ
koṭy-aṁśo 'py asya na syāt tad api
guṇa-gaṇo yaḥ svataḥ-siddha āste
śrīmac-caitanyacandra-priya-caraṇa-
nakha-jyotir āmoda-bhājām

"Persons who are attached to the rays of the effulgent nails on the toes of the lotus feet of the beloved and dear devotees of Lord Caitanya are by themselves fully qualified with all transcendental qualities. Even powerful renunciation, equanimity, sense control, fortitude, meditation, and similar other great qualities that are found in the devotees of Viṣṇu do not compare to even one-millionth of a part of their transcendental attributes."

Real Wealth

The general masses who are driven by the dictates of the mind for material enjoyment, desire to accumulate more and more wealth, which is the medium for obtaining their sense gratification. However, by pure transcendental intellect, one can objectively assess the value of material wealth and see that there is no wealth that can be compared with the value of love for Rādhā and Kṛṣṇa. Here are some quotations in support of the above conception from the *śāstra*:

kim alabhyaṁ bhagavati
prasanne śrī-niketane
tathāpi tat-parā rājan
na hi vāñchanti kiñcana

"Although everything is available for devotees of the Personality of Godhead, they do not desire anything for their own sense enjoyment." (*Bhāg*. 10.39.2)

mām anārādhya duḥkhārtaḥ
kuṭumbāsakta-mānasaḥ
sat-saṅga-rahito martyo
vṛddha-sevā-paricyutaḥ

"Conditioned souls are always unhappy in their attachment for relatives as they do not worship Me and are thus bereft of the association of pure devotees and service unto Me."

sva-jivanādhikaṁ prārthyaṁ
śrī-viṣṇu-jana-saṅgataḥ
vicchedena kṣaṇaṁ cātra
na sukhāṁśaṁ labhāmahe

"The association of the devotees of Viṣṇu is worth more than my life, because being detached from such association for a moment, I do not feel even the slightest trace of happiness." (*Bṛhad-bhāgavatāmṛta* 1.5.44)

muktānām api siddhānāṁ
nārāyaṇa-parāyaṇaḥ
sudurlabhaḥ praśāntātmā
koṭiṣv api mahāmune

"Out of millions of great sages who are liberated souls, it is very difficult to find a sober devotee of Lord Nārāyaṇa." (*Bhāg*. 6.14.5)

anugrahāya bhūtānāṁ
mānuṣaṁ deham āsthitaḥ
bhajate tādṛśīḥ krīḍā
yāḥ śrutvā tat-paro bhavet

"The Personality of Godhead, in order to bestow mercy upon His devotees, appears on this earth and manifests His pastimes so that the devotees may be attracted to Him and His pastimes." (*Bhāg*. 10.33.37)

ata ātyantikaṁ kṣemaṁ
pṛcchāmo bhavato 'naghāḥ
saṁsāre 'smin kṣaṇārdho 'pi
sat-saṅgaḥ śevadhir nṛṇām

"O most auspicious one, I am asking You for the highest benediction. I wish to have the association of Your pure devotees because the association of Your devotees for even a moment is the most valuable gain in this world." (*Bhāg*. 11.2.28)

tasmāt sarvātmanā rājan
hariḥ sarvatra sarvadā
śrotavyaḥ kīrtitavyaś ca
smartavyo bhagavān nṛṇām

"O King, the Personality of Godhead Hari is to be heard, glorified, and remembered by all human beings at all times, in all places, and in all circumstances." (*Bhāg*. 2.2.36)

tasmād ekena manasā
bhagavān sātvatāṁ patiḥ
śrotavyaḥ kīrtitavyaś ca
dhyeyaḥ pūjyaś ca nityadā

"The Personality of Godhead, who is the sustainer of the pure devotees, is to be heard and glorified, worshiped and meditated upon with rapt attention at all times." (*Bhāg*. 1.2.14)

āsām aho caraṇa-reṇu-juṣām ahaṁ syāṁ
vṛndāvane kim api gulma-latauṣadhīnām
yā dustyajaṁ svajanam ārya-pathaṁ ca hitvā
bhejur mukunda-padavīṁ śrutibhir vimṛgyām

"My desire is to become a blade of grass or a creeper that grows in the forest of Vraja. In that way, it will be possible for me to receive the dust of the feet of those great personalities who have worshiped the lotus feet of the great liberator, Mukunda. The dust of the feet of these great personalities is sought after even by the *śrutis*. Leaving aside the affection of their own kith and kin, which is ordinarily impossible to give up, the *gopīs* of Vraja have sacrificed everything for the satisfaction of Śrī Kṛṣṇa." (*Bhāg*. 10.47.61)

vikrīḍitaṁ vraja-vadhūbhir idaṁ ca viṣṇoḥ
śraddhānvito 'nuśṛṇuyād atha varṇayed yaḥ
bhaktiṁ parāṁ bhagavati pratilabhya kāmaṁ
hṛd-rogam āśv apahinoty acireṇa dhīraḥ

"A person who with a reverential attitude hears the transcendental pastimes of Śrī Kṛṣṇa with the damsels of Vraja from the mouth of a pure devotee and then describes those pastimes accordingly, achieves the supramundane loving service of Godhead within no time and thereby drives away mundane lusty desires for sense gratification from his heart." (*Bhāg.* 10.33.40)

etāvān eva loke 'smin
puṁsāṁ dharmaḥ paraḥ smṛtaḥ
bhakti-yogo bhagavati
tan-nāma-grahaṇādibhiḥ

"The highest duty of every human being in this world is to be engaged in the loving service of the Personality of Godhead and to chant His Holy Name." (*Bhāg.* 6.3.22)

Dry, speculative knowledge is compared to the bitter fruits of the Nīm tree. This fruit is unworthy of human consumption but is quite suitable for those persons who, like the crows, are situated in a rough, argumentative way of life. Their dry philosophical speculations sound like the crowing of crows.

On the other hand, the newly-bloomed buds of the mango fruit, which are sweet to taste and completely palatable, are compared to the transcendental loving service of Godhead. As such, this fruit is tasted by the pure devotees of Śrī Kṛṣṇa, who are compared to the parrots who are always delivering sweet sounds. Dry philosophical speculation is the only gain of the unfortunate *jñānī* empiric philosopher, and the juicy nectarean taste of the loving service of Godhead is the drink of the fortunate devotees.

Thus Lord Caitanya and Rāmānanda Rāya again passed the whole night in the transcendental joy of talking about Śrī Kṛṣṇa and His pastimes. Sometimes they wept and sometimes they danced while absorbed in ecstatic trance, and in this way the night came to an end. In the morning, both Rāmānanda and Lord Caitanya parted to attend to their respective duties, and in the evening they again met together as on the previous night.

Enlightening the Heart

After talking for a few minutes, Rāmānanda fell at the feet of Lord Caitanya and submitted his heartfelt realization:

eta tattva mora citte kaile prakāśana
brahmāke veda yena paḍāila nārāyaṇa
antaryāmī īśvarera ei rīti haye
bāhire nā kahe, vastu prakāśe hṛdaye

"My Lord, You have enlightened my heart with various truths and made me able to express them as the fundamental knowledge of Rādhā and Kṛṣṇa, the essence of divine love. Previously, you similarly enlightened the heart of Brahmā with Vedic knowledge. The Lord who is the constant companion of the living being as the Supersoul does all this out of His unbounded causeless mercy. He does not appear face-to-face outwardly, but He enlightens one from within."

In the *Bhagavad-gītā,* this is confirmed. The Personality of Godhead says that in order to show special favor to His devotee, He enlightens the heart of the devotee and drives away the darkness of ignorance by the illumination of transcendental knowledge. And in the very beginning of the beautiful *Śrīmad-Bhāgavatam* (1.1.1), the following important statement is made:

janmādy asya yato 'nvayād itarataś cārteṣv abhijñaḥ svarāṭ
tene brahma hṛdā ya ādi-kavaye muhyanti yat sūrayaḥ

tejo-vāri-mṛdāṁ yathā vinimayo yatra tri-sargo 'mṛṣā
dhāmnā svena sadā nirasta-kuhakaṁ satyaṁ paraṁ dhīmahi

"The Absolute Truth, the Personality of Godhead, is the only independent self-sufficient King of all living entities. It is He only who enlightened the heart of Brahmā, who is the original poet and singer of the Vedic hymns. It is He only about whom all kinds of empiric scholars become bewildered at every moment. In Him only is the combination of the five elements earth, fire, water, air, and ether possible. And it is He alone who is recognized as the true source of the internal energy, the external energy, and the marginal energy.

"Let us therefore pray for shelter under the lotus feet of Śrī Kṛṣṇa, who is free from all illusions by dint of His own energy and who is the Absolute Truth. This Absolute Truth is ascertained as the fountainhead of pure knowledge in all the affairs of creation, maintenance, and annihilation. This is the only logical conclusion to be drawn after carefully understanding the subject either directly or indirectly."

I Have One Doubt

Rāmānanda Rāya then petitioned the Lord,

eka saṁśaya mora āchaye hṛdaye
kṛpā kari' kaha more tāhāra niścaye
pahile dekhiluṅ tomāra sannyāsi-svarūpa
ebe tomā dekhi muñi śyāma-gopa-rūpa
tomāra sammukhe dekhi kāñcana-pañcālikā
tāṅra gaura-kāntye tomāra sarva aṅga ḍhākā
tāhāte prakaṭa dekhoṅ sa-vaṁśī vadana
nānā bhāve cañcala tāhe kamala-nayana

ei-mata tomā dekhi' haya camatkāra
akapaṭe kaha, prabhu, kāraṇa ihāra

"My Lord, I have but one doubt within my heart, and I hope You will kindly remove it by Your grace. At first I saw You appear like a *sannyāsī,* but now I am seeing You as Śyāmasundara, the cowherd boy. I now see You appearing like a golden doll, and Your entire body appears covered by a golden luster. I see that You are holding a flute to Your mouth, and Your lotus eyes are moving very restlessly due to various ecstasies. I actually see You in this way, and this is very wonderful. My Lord, please tell me without duplicity what is causing this"

The Lord replied that those who are deeply absorbed in a loving relationship with Kṛṣṇa are all first-class devotees. As a result of their natural love of Godhead, they realize the presence of their worshipful Lord Śrī Kṛṣṇa everywhere, as they look upon all varieties of moving and nonmoving objects. The objects of their observation do not appear before them as they are, but they appear differently in relationship with Śrī Kṛṣṇa. Here are some quotations in this regard from the *Śrīmad-Bhāgavatam.*

sarva-bhūteṣu yaḥ paśyed
bhagavad-bhāvam ātmanaḥ
bhūtāni bhagavaty ātmany
eṣa bhāgavatottamaḥ

"The first-class devotee perceives everywhere the presence of Śrī Kṛṣṇa, who is the life of all lives, and in Śrī Kṛṣṇa they perceive the presence of all animate and inanimate objects." *(Bhāg.*11.2.45)

vana-latās tarava ātmani viṣṇuṁ
vyañjayantya iva puṣpa-phalāḍhyāḥ

praṇata-bhāra-viṭapā madhu-dhārāḥ
prema-hṛṣṭa-tanavo vavṛṣuḥ sma

"The jungle trees and creepers full with their fruits and flowers bowed before the Lord with feelings that Śrī Kṛṣṇa is their vital life. In a mood of transcendental cheerfulness and ecstatic joy, the trees and creepers poured forth large amounts of honey in His presence. This was possible due to their pure love of Godhead." (*Bhāg.* 10.35.9)

Lord Caitanya continued to speak:

rādhā-kṛṣṇe tomāra mahā-prema haya
yāhāṅ tāhāṅ rādhā-kṛṣṇa tomāre sphuraya

"You have deep regard for Rādhā and Kṛṣṇa, and as such you can perceive Their presence anywhere and everywhere."

Rāmānanda Rāya was not, however, satisfied at heart with this answer given by Lord Caitanya, although the words of the Lord were certainly correct according to *śāstra.* Thus he said,

raya kahe—prabhu tumi chāḍa bhāri-bhūri
mora āge nija-rūpa nā kariha curi
rādhikāra bhāva-kānti kari' angīkāra
nija-rasa āsvādite kariyācha avatāra
nija-gūḍha-kārya tomāra—prema āsvādana
ānuṣaṅge prema-maya kaile tribhuvana
āpane āile more karite uddhāra
ebe kapaṭa kara—tomāra kona vyavahāra

"My Lord, please give up this roundabout way of revealing Your true personality. Kindly do not try to hide Your real identity. I know who You are: You are Śrī Kṛṣṇa Himself covered by the complexion of

Śrīmatī Rādhārāṇī. You have descended to relish the ecstasy of Your transcendental pastimes with Her. The main purpose of Your appearance is to relish the feelings of Your devotees' love for You and simultaneously to distribute that love throughout the three worlds. You have come to me out of Your own accord, so how is it that You want to hide Yourself now?"

Lord Caitanya Revealed

At this, Lord Caitanya smiled and revealed Himself as Rasarāja, the King of all divine *rasas*, and also as His other Self, Śrīmatī Rādhārāṇī, who is Mahābhāva, love of Godhead personified. Then He revealed Himself in one form as the unity of the Divine Couple—Śrī Kṛṣṇa appearing with the sentiment and color of Śrīmatī Rādhārāṇī.

rādhā kṛṣṇa-praṇaya-vikṛtir hlādinī śaktir asmād
ekātmānāv api bhuvi purā deha-bhedaṁ gatau tau
caitanyākhyaṁ prakaṭam adhunā tad-dvayaṁ caikyam āptaṁ
rādhā-bhāva-dyuti-suvalitaṁ naumi kṛṣṇa-svarūpam

"The loving affairs of Rādhā and Kṛṣṇa are transcendental manifestations of the Lord's internal pleasure-giving potency. Although Rādhā and Kṛṣṇa are one in Their identity, They separated Themselves eternally. Now these two transcendental personalities have again united in the form of Śrī Kṛṣṇa Caitanya. I bow down to Him, who has manifested Himself with the sentiment and complexion of Śrīmatī Rādhārāṇī although He is Kṛṣṇa Himself."

Lord Caitanya revealed Himself as the one that is two and the two that are one. This is a most unique manifestation of the Absolute Truth. Only those who are fortunate enough to know Śrī Kṛṣṇa

Caitanya, as well as Śrī Śrī Rādhā-Kṛṣṇa, by the grace of Rāmānanda Rāya, can serve the eternal forms that have united in one.

Rāmānanda Rāya fainted in ecstasy upon seeing the unique manifestation of the divine form of Lord Caitanya, and he became overwhelmed with transcendental emotion. In a swoon, he collapsed to the ground.

At that moment, Lord Caitanya touched the body of Rāmānanda and brought him back to his external senses. Rāmānanda was again astonished to see Lord Caitanya in the form of a *sannyāsī*. The Lord then embraced Rāmānanda and pacified him by saying that other than Rāmānanda Rāya, nobody had ever seen that transcendentally combined form.

Lord Caitanya said that nothing is unknown to Rāmānanda Rāya about His pastimes, and as such He showed him the unique manifestation of His form.

gaura aṅga nahe mora—rādhāṅga-sparśana
gopendra-suta vinā teṅho nā sparśe anya-jana
tāṅra bhāve bhāvita kari' ātma-mana
tabe nija-mādhurya kari āsvādana
tomāra ṭhāñi āmāra kichu gupta nāhi karma
lukāile prema-bale jāna sarva-marma
gupte rākhiha, kāhāṅ nā kario prakāśa
āmāra bātula-ceṣṭā loke upahāsa
āmi—eka bātula, tumi—dvitīya bātula
ataeva tomāya āmāya ha-i sama-tula

"O Rāmānanda, I am not merely a person of fair complexion appearing before you. I am the selfsame personality Śrī Kṛṣṇa and I eternally exhibit this form, which is imbued with the bodily hue of Śrīmati Rādhārāṇī. Nobody can touch Śrīmati Rādhārāṇī except Śrī Kṛṣṇa. Therefore I adorn Myself with the sentiments of Śrīmatī Rādhārāṇī and thereby enjoy Myself. In this eternal form of Mine, I also relish the sweetness of Śrī Kṛṣṇa. But please do not disclose this secret of mine! Ordinary men may laugh at Me in my mad attempt. In this matter, I am certainly the number one madman and you are number two. And as both of us are in the same category, there is no difference between yourself and Myself."

A Mine of Nectar

The Lord thus enjoyed the company of Rāmānanda Rāya while discussing about Śrī Kṛṣṇa continuously for ten days. Those conversations that took place between Rāmānanda Rāya and Lord Caitanya were very, very confidential talks about Vraja-dhāma, the place where the transcendental pastimes of Śrīmatī Rādhārāṇī and Śrī Kṛṣṇa are eternally manifest. In those conversations, the ecstasy that flows in Vraja-dhāma was thoroughly discussed. There were also many other talks between Rāmānanda and Lord Caitanya, which are impossible for anyone to understand. In short, the whole topic was just like a mine of gemlike information, which produced one gem after another for the benefit of all humankind. The mine of that conversation is compared to an unfathomed, deep metallic reservoir. As the mine was being excavated, precious metals of different categories came out in the form of copper, bell metal, silver, gold, and lastly touchstone.

Precious metals were excavated both in the preliminary as well as the concluding discussions between Rāmānanda Rāya and Lord Caitanya. In the preliminary talks, *In Search of the Ultimate Goal of Life*, the idea of following the moral and social divisions of society is compared to copper, the mother of metals. The idea of offering the results of one's work to Śrī Kṛṣṇa (*karma-yoga)* is compared to bell metal. The idea of renouncing the world and taking *karma-sannyāsa* is compared to silver. The idea of devotional service mixed with empiric speculative knowledge *(jñāna-miśrā-bhakti)* is compared to gold, and lastly, devotional service unmixed with any empiric knowledge (*jñāna-śūnya-bhakti*) is compared to touchstone.

In the concluding discussions, the same comparison is made in regard to the different transcendental sentiments of devotional service. The conception of *dāsya-premā* is compared to copper, *sakhya-premā* to bell metal, *vātsalya-premā* to silver, and *mādhurya-premā* to gold. And lastly the transcendental pastimes of Śrī Śrī Rādhā-Kṛṣṇa are compared to touchstone.

Entrance into the above-mentioned touchstone of *jñāna-śūnya-bhakti* can be obtained by the persevering devotee who has the necessary energy, fortitude, good association, and honesty of purpose. With all these necessary qualifications, that touchstone is easily available.

The next day, Lord Caitanya asked permission from Rāmānanda Rāya to continue on His tour of South India. The Lord also requested him to follow His instruction, advising him as follows:

viṣaya chāḍiyā tumi yāha nīlācale
āmi tīrtha kari' tāṅhā āsiba alpa-kāle
dui-jane nīlācale rahiba eka-saṅge
sukhe goṅāiba kāla kṛṣṇa-kathā-raṅge

"Please go to Nīlācala (Jagannātha Purī), resigning from your worldly activities. I will arrive there very shortly after finishing My tour. We will stay at Nīlācala together and pass our time in great happiness by our talks about the transcendental pastimes of Rādhā and Kṛṣṇa."

Saying this, Lord Caitanya embraced Rāmānanda and sent him to his home, and then He Himself went to take rest for the night.

The next morning, Lord Caitanya visited the local temple of Hanumān, paid His respects to the Deity, and then left to travel throughout South India.

During the presence of Lord Caitanya at Vidyānagara, the city where Rāmānanda Rāya lived, all the scholars of different schools of philosophy were converted into devotees of Śrī Kṛṣṇa, and they gave up their previous ways of thinking. After the departure of Lord Caitanya, Rāmānanda was overwhelmed with grief on account of separation from the Lord, and thus he remained aloof from all sorts of routine work while continuing to absorb himself in deep meditation on the Lord.

This is a short sketch of the meeting that took place between Rāmānanda Rāya and Śrī Caitanya Mahāprabhu. The instructive and transcendental topics that were discussed between them are completely sublime and simple at the same time. Any fortunate person can take advantage of the revelations within this conversation and thus bring about the perfection of his life. Once the topic is heard with a reverential attitude, it will no longer be possible to leave aside the spiritual ambition of reaching the abode of Rādhā and Kṛṣṇa.

By hearing this short narration, one can enter into the essence of transcendental romance and pure love of Godhead. The most important thing to understand from this discussion is the secret of Lord Caitanya's appearance in this world and the essence of His *saṅkīrtana* movement.

Faith

Only the faithful can enter into the intricacies of these topics, and faith is the basic principle for making progress in the supramental state of transcendental love in separation. The *līlā* of

Rādhā and Kṛṣṇa is transcendental and confidential. One who has faith in Lord Caitanya and His recommended process for spiritual upliftment can enter into the confidential service of the Divine Couple, which is all-attractive for the pure devotees.

It must be understood that the talks between Lord Caitanya and Rāmānanda Rāya are not a creation of mental speculators who are not in the transcendental chain of disciplic succession and who are always doubtful about the Absolute Truth. Nobody whose basic tendency is to engage in mundane arguments can enter the precincts of these topics. They are above such a materialistic approach. Because the subject matter is supramundane, it is therefore not possible to understand it without having reached the supramental state.

Nobody need try to understand these transcendental topics by strenuous academic manipulation of the brain and mind, because both the mundane brain and mind are useless when attempting to reach this supramental state. Only service to Godhead and His agents can help one to experience the revelation of the truth. Mental speculation, which produces only pseudoresults, simply creates a disturbance.

The transcendental domain discussed by Śrī Rāmānanda Rāya and Lord Caitanya is solely the property of those faithful devotees of Śrī Kṛṣṇa who have a record of service in devotional life.

All glories to Lord Caitanya and Lord Nityānanda Prabhu along with Śrī Advaita Prabhu and all the devotees of Lord Caitanya, who are known as the *Gaura-bhaktas*. Lord Caitanya, by the disc weapon of His exclusive mercy, delivered the inhabitants of South India, who were situated like elephants being attacked by the crocodiles of different religious sects. Thus Lord Caitanya converted them all to Vaiṣṇavism and proceeded onward throughout South India, where He visited many, many holy places of pilgrimage.

PRONOUNCIATION GUIDE

The system of transliteration used in this book conforms to a system that scholars have accepted to indicate the pronunciation of each sound in the Sanskrit and Bengali language.

The short vowel **a** is pronounced like the **u** in but, but long **ā** like the **a** in f**a**r. Short **i** is pronounced as in p**i**n, long **ī** as in p**i**que, short **u** as in p**u**ll, and long **ū** as in r**u**le.

The vowel **ṛ** is pronounced like the **ri** in **ri**m, **e** and **ai** are pronounced as the **ey** in th**ey**, and **o** and **au** are pronounced as the **o** in g**o**.

The *anusvāra* (**ṁ**), which is a pure nasal sound, is pronounced like the **n** in the French word bo**n**, and *visarga* (**ḥ**), which is a strong aspirate, is pronounced as a final **h** sound. At the end of a couplet **aḥ** is pronounced like **aha**, and **iḥ** like **ihi**.

The guttural consonants -**k**, **kh**, **g**, **gh**, and **ṇ** - are pronounced from the throat in much the same manner as in English. **K** is pronounced as in **k**ite, **kh** as in Ec**kh**art, **g** as in **g**ive, **gh** as in di**g h**ard, and **ṇ** as in si**ng**.

The palatal consonants - **c**, **ch**, **j**, **jh**, and **ñ** are pronounced from the palate with the middle of the tongue. **C** is pronounced as in **ch**air, **ch** as in staun**ch-h**eart, **j** as in **j**oy, **jh** as in he**dgeh**og, and **ñ** as in ca**ny**on.

The celebral consonants - **ṭ**, **ṭh**, **ḍ**, **ḍh**, and **ṇ** are pronounced with the tip of the tongue turned up and drawn back against the dome of the palate. **Ṭ** is pronounced as in **t**ub, **ṭh** as in ligh**t-h**eart, **ḍ** as in **d**ove, **ḍh** as in re**d-h**ot, and **ṇ** as in **n**ut.

The dental consonants - **t**, **th**, **d**, **dh**, and **n** are pronounced in the same manner as the celebrals, but with the forepart of the tongue against the teeth.

The labial consonants - **p**, **ph**, **b**, **bh**, and **m** are pronounced with the lips. **P** is pronounced as in **p**ine, **ph** as in u**ph**ill, **b** as in **b**ird, **bh** as in ru**b-h**ard, and **m** as in **m**other.

The semivowels - **y**, **r**, **l**, and **v** are pronounced as in **y**es, **r**un, **l**ight, and **v**ine respectively. The sibilants - **ś**, **ṣ** and **s** - are pronounced, respectively as in the German word **s**prechen and the English word **sh**ine and **s**un.

The letter **h** is pronounced as in **h**ome.

VERSE INDEX